BIG SHOTS

BIG SHOTS

THE MEN
BEHIND
THE BOOZE

★

A. J. Baime

NEW AMERICAN LIBRARY

New American Library
Published by New American Library, a division of
Penguin Group (USA) Inc., 375 Hudson Street,
New York, New York 10014, U.S.A.
Penguin Books Ltd, 80 Strand,
London WC2R 0RL, England
Penguin Books Australia Ltd, 250 Camberwell Road,
Camberwell, Victoria 3124, Australia
Penguin Books Canada Ltd, 10 Alcorn Avenue,
Toronto, Ontario, Canada M4V 3B2
Penguin Books (N.Z.) Ltd, Cnr Rosedale and Airborne Roads,
Albany, Auckland 1310, New Zealand

Penguin Books Ltd, Registered Offices:
80 Strand, London WC2R 0RL, England

First published by New American Library,
a division of Penguin Group (USA) Inc.

First Printing, November 2003
10   9   8   7   6   5   4   3   2

REGISTERED TRADEMARK—MARCA REGISTRADA

Library of Congress Cataloging-in-Publication Data

Baime, Albert J.
Big shots : the men behind the booze / Albert Baime.
p.   cm.
ISBN 0-451-20980-X
1. Liquors.   I. Title.
TP597.B25   2003
641.2'55—dc21   2003008023

Set in Humanist
Designed by Erin Benach

Printed in the United States of America

BOOKS ARE AVAILABLE AT QUANTITY DISCOUNTS WHEN USED TO
PROMOTE PRODUCTS OR SERVICES. FOR INFORMATION PLEASE WRITE
TO PREMIUM MARKETING DIVISION, PENGUIN GROUP (USA) INC.,
375 HUDSON STREET, NEW YORK, NEW YORK 10014.

Bar menu

A Note on the Text

This is a book about liquor. Though it was difficult, to say the least, I've omitted beer and wine, with the notable exception of Dom Perignon, whose fascinating story I couldn't ignore, and a short chapter on Martini & Rossi vermouth. A good portion of this book is about whiskey—American, Scotch, Canadian, Irish. To make matters easy, I've blown off the whiskey/whisky controversy, simply because no one really cares that much. And if you do, you should pour yourself a whiskey to take your mind off things. Throughout the book, the profiles of these men and their liquors are garnished with any number of cocktail recipes. Unless otherwise noted, these recipes have been distilled down from the million different available sources to suit my liking. In other words, the mixology is an informed suggestion. Try each recipe out, and tinker with them as you like.

Introduction

> You cannot drown yourself in drink. I've tried. You float.
> —John Barrymore

About twelve thousand years ago, or maybe closer to two hundred thousand years ago (who knows for sure?), someone discovered alcohol—by mistake. To this person, whoever he or she is, a toast should be raised, especially considering the strange particulars of how it probably went down. There are any number of theories, but the following is the most plausible:

It was a broiling hot day in the Mideast—very likely in what is presently Iran—and some tribesmen were foraging for fruit. They liked grapes in particular. The wild fruit balls were colorful and seductive, bunches of little orbs that exploded with sweet juice when you bit down on them, each with a seed that assured there would be more to eat tomorrow. As they toiled, the tribesmen grew thirsty. The sun burned above them like the sizzling yolk of a giant egg frying in the sky. Their lips cracked, and their tongues hung out of their mouths. Water was a scarce commodity. There wasn't enough to go around, and every drop counted.

At the end of the day, the tribesmen retired to where they kept their fruit. Tired and thirsty, one noticed that, in a large container filled with grapes, the weight of the pile had crushed the fruit at the bottom, and some juice had leaked out. The man reached down and scooped up some of the juice using a container of some sort, perhaps a cup whittled out of wood. First he sniffed the juice. The stuff gave off a strange smell—sickly sweet and pungent. There might've been insects crawling in it. But the guy was thirsty, so he sipped nervously.

And then he sipped again. And again. Seeing that it was safe, he gulped down the whole lot.

Slowly a tender feeling began to overcome him. The tight sinews in his neck and back began to relax. A strange numbness spread into his limbs, as if tiny spiders were crawling through his veins. He felt dizzy—a soft, warm buzz. Hours later, he was busted for driving a stolen car while intoxicated, with a cross-dresser in the passenger seat who was later identified as Winston Churchill, the greatest drunk of all time.

Thus alcohol as we know it was born. Or that's my version anyway. There is at least one more commonly accepted theory—that a woman, a member of the harem of an ancient mythological Persian king named Jemsheed, discovered alcohol. Apparently, this king loved grapes so much that he collected and preserved them. Some of the grapes rotted, turned to mush, and fermented. Seeing that the fruit had turned sour, the king placed it in a vessel, labeled it poison, and lodged it in a vault. (Why he didn't just throw it out is anyone's guess.) Later, one of his harem, while suffering from a devastating migraine, drank some of the poison in hopes of killing herself. After she drank the grape juice, the headache disappeared and the woman was overcome by a strange ecstasy. According to the legend, the king caught on and began cultivating grapes for wine production. To this day, wine in the Mideast is sometimes referred to as *zeher-e-khoosh*, or the delightful poison.

Whichever theory you accept, the facts remain the same. The dust on the fruit had yeast in it. When the fruit rotted, the natural sugars had mingled with the yeast on the skins and the juice had fermented—literally turned from water into wine.

From that moment in the Neolithic Period onward, ethyl alcohol (C_2H_5OH) would become a staple in nearly every burgeoning civilization across the globe. Later on, in the twelfth century (though some argue it was much earlier), European monks would have the bright idea to boil wine and collect the vapors—a process known as distillation. Since alcohol vaporizes at a lower temperature than water, the monks realized it was possible to separate it from other ingredients, to concentrate its strength. Then the fun *really* began.

It's no coincidence that, as different cultures around the world discovered the alchemy of distillation, many chose the same name for their drinks. The monks of the Dark Ages in Europe named their distilled spirits *aqua vitae*—"water of life" in Latin. Early Scottish distillers called whiskey *usquebaugh*—"water of life" in Gaelic. The Poles called their liquor *shiznennia vodka*—"water of life" in Slavic. The French called brandy *eau-de-vie*. You get the point. Wherever knowledge spread, alcohol followed, made out of whatever ingredients were on hand.

Now jump forward a few hundred years. You're standing in a bar in the twenty-first century, staring at liquor bottles, tapping your foot to a Johnny Cash tune. Spread out before you are myriad drink choices: rums, vodkas, whiskies, gins, tequilas. Some are as clear as water; others are the color of polished copper, amber brown, or a gold so rich it looks as if the sun had melted into a bottle. The exotic liquids come from all four corners of the earth, different nectars exuding different flavors and scents, with brand names and marketing slogans written in strange tongues. You ask yourself, how did drinking go from the "water of life" days to the bizarre mix of branded mass-marketed stuff we drink today?

It's an epic story, the history of booze. The evolution of liquor is a story about love and war, rape and murder, miraculous wealth and abject poverty. It's a story about the conquest of economies and political revolutions, CIA assassination plots, earthquakes, plagues, piracy, and vomiting. The story's main characters are the proverbial men behind the bar. Jack Daniel. Johnnie Walker. Jose Cuervo. Captain Henry Morgan. Don Facundo Bacardi Masso. Some of these men made tons of liquor and didn't drink much. At least one didn't make any at all, but drank himself to death. (Can you guess which?) All of them had one thing in common: they adored alcohol, each in his own way.

The following narrative tells the story of booze from the early days to the present, through a series of profiles about the guys on the bottles, and the companies they created. Each chapter tells the story of a man wrapped up in the turmoil of his time, and collectively, you get the whole story of alcohol post-Shakespeare. From the rum-addled pirates who raped and pillaged the Caribbean to the Prohibition-era rumrunners who smuggled Canadian whiskey over the border here in the States, the history of liquor presents one beautifully picaresque tale after another. If nothing else, you'll be the most enlightened person in the bar. And that's worth drinking to.

But really, in the end, this book is about getting to know your booze and learning about its past. A person's drink is kind of like a spouse. If you abuse your drink, it'll make your life hell. (Alcohol kills about two million people every year, and though drink tends to make you feel no pain, killing yourself with it is a rough way to go.) If you treat your drink with respect and curiosity, the relationship can grow for a lifetime. The more you know about your drink, the better each drop tastes. And like a spouse, there's a secret to keeping it happy.

Every now and then, lean over and give it a little kiss. It'll reward you every time.

PART I

AMERICAN WHISKEY MEN

CHAPTER 1

JIM BEAM

EST. BIG SHOTS

The Granddaddy of Bourbon and
the Grandson Who Just Might
Have Murdered Him

Hey, who took the cork off my lunch?
—W.C. Fields, date unknown

"**G**oddamn! Hell! We're gonna be late!" cries seventy-three-year-old Booker "Hard Times" Noe, the master distiller emeritus of Jim Beam's stable of whiskeys, his giant body shoehorned into the front passenger's seat of a sea green Ford minivan.

"Do you want to put your seat belt on?" asks the driver, a young, dark-haired guy named Jim.

"I don't mind if you can manage to get the thing around me," Booker replies in his trademark deep Kentucky drawl. Jim gives the old man's six-foot-four-inch frame the once-over (Booker looks like he's just swallowed a bourbon barrel whole), ponders for about three seconds, then throws the car in gear and hits the gas. We're headed from the main Jim Beam distillery in Clermont, Kentucky, fifty miles away to Wild Turkey in Lawrenceburg, where a ceremony will be held to induct, among nine others, the original Jim Beam into the Bourbon Hall of Fame. Booker will be accepting the award in honor of his grandfather. (The so-called Bourbon Hall of Fame is just a couple years old. Like a lot of things in these parts, it's basically an excuse to indulge in a Kentucky double feature: whiskey and ham.)

Slowly the minivan pulls down the road past the Beam distillery on the right: a massive operation of pipes slithering like petrified snakes out of the ground with giant stacks blowing smoke and trucks loading up with cases upon cases of some of the finest bourbon in Kentucky. The stink of mash fermenting assaults the nose. To the left, towering corrugated metal rack houses hold thousands of fifty-three-gallon five-hundred-pound barrels of Beam whiskey: Jim Beam White Label, Jim Beam Black, plus the company's four "small batch" bottlings (Basil Hayden, Baker's, Knob Creek, and Booker's). In the front seat, dressed in a classic dark suit, Booker Noe himself smiles when he sees the rack houses, the hot Kentucky sun bouncing rays off his bald head. On the classic Beam White Label bottle, Booker's name is listed at the bottom as master distiller, under his grandfather's name. He's been making whiskey for fifty years, truly (and pardon the cliché) a legend in his own time.

"The last time I went to Wild Turkey ten years ago," Booker says, "I was with Jimmy Russell [Turkey's master distiller]. He says I got drunk. I say *he* got drunk. *Goddamn! We all got drunk!*"

At the wheel, Jim checks his watch and squirms nervously as we merge onto the Bluegrass Highway, in the heart of what is fondly called "the Bourbon Trail." Looks like we're running late. Booker appears nervous, as if the revelers might suck the entire Wild Turkey distillery dry before we get there.

"Now where was I?" he asks. He was telling a story about Jim Beam, his grandfather, and the last time he saw him alive. As the story goes, Booker says, he believes he might have killed his grandfather. That's right: killed him.

"This is the God's truth. Every word. Hell, I remember it like it was yesterday. It was December 25, 1947. I'd shot some birds, and I took these quail over to give my grandfather for Christmas. He was in bed, sick. I gave him the birds. My grandmother, his wife, asked him if it would be okay if she gave me his shotgun. He said yes, so she went and got this old gun, a Model 12 Winchester pump shotgun. It rolled seven shot, but you could only put three in there by law. During Prohibition, my grandfather was, among other things, a coal miner, and he used the gun to guard the mines. Anyway, I gave him the birds and he gave me the shotgun. That was Christmas Day.

"On the twenty-seventh, he was dead in bed," Booker continues, "just like he was sleeping. Now I don't know for sure, but I think he ate those birds. . . ."

Sounds like murder, right? More like manslaughter.

For the rest of the drive to Lawrenceburg for Jim Beam's induction into the Bourbon Hall of Fame (a drive that took a little longer than expected because of a few wrong turns), Booker Noe continued telling stories that, collectively, piece together the life of his grandfather—stories about making Jim Beam whiskey, about Prohibition and Kentucky moonshiners, about the growth of the largest bourbon distillery in the world and more. With a whole bunch of gaps filled in (Booker's memory gets foggy here and there), the following is a brief life of one of the greatest whiskey men in history, and the strange world of American distillers he was born into.

By the time the original Jim Beam kicked off his distilling career, whiskey was already a staple "resource" in Kentucky. When the first settlers came to the New World, they brought with them a distaste for "strong water." (They were Puritans.) The original colonies in Massachusetts and New York were dry. But the Irish and Scottish settlers who came at the beginning of the eighteenth century had a taste for grain spirit, and they knew very well how to make it. They settled in what is now Maryland, Pennsylvania, Tennessee, and Virginia—states with fertile soil where rye grew plentifully.

All the ingredients necessary to make good whiskey were on hand: grain, pure water, forests to provide wood for lighting a fire under the still. By 1776, when the United States was born, smoke columns were rising off stills throughout the western part of the country.

The first Homestead Act offered free land grants to anyone with the guts to head west and settle in the wilderness. Among other places, thousands of pioneers of Scotch-Irish descent from Pennsylvania settled in Kentucky County, Virginia, where corn grew. Naturally, the settlers started making whiskey out of the grain, and they soon figured out that corn whiskey was much sweeter and arguably more full-flavored than rye. Have yourself a taste test of Jim Beam bourbon (bourbon must be at least 51 percent corn whiskey by law) and Jim Beam rye (with the yellow label) and you'll be able to tell for yourself.

As Bill Samuels Jr., president of Maker's Mark Distillery in Loretto, Kentucky, put it: "The fact that the native grain of Kentucky was Indian maize changed one of the key distinguishing elements between bourbon whiskey as we know it and other whiskeys."

Eventually, distilleries sprang up around a particular section of what is now Kentucky where a thin layer of soil covered a huge limestone shelf. The limestone gave the water a particularly fresh flavor—great for making whiskey. (This same limestone is responsible for the state's famous blue grass, which is rich in calcium and said to have given rise to the premium breed of Thoroughbred horses raised on it. It's no coincidence that the greatest horse race in the nation is run in Kentucky.)

By the end of the eighteenth century, some two thousand small distilleries were operating in Kentucky. Among the early distillers, some have bourbons named after them that you can buy in stores today: Elijah Craig, a Baptist minister, the first to notice the fine flavor and caramel color whiskey gained when aged in charred oak barrels (according to legend, Craig used herring barrels, and the charring removed the fish odor); Evan Williams, a Welshman who established Kentucky's first commercial distillery on Main Street in Louisville in 1783; Scot James Crow of Old Crow fame; and Jacob Beam, Jim's great-grandfather, a distiller of German descent who sold his first barrel of whiskey in 1795.

Kentucky became the fifteenth state in 1792, and its fledgling government named one county after the French royal family—the Bourbons—in recognition of the support they gave to the Americans during the war against England. (There's also a Louisville and a Versailles in Kentucky.) The whiskey made in Bourbon County had a strong reputation, and drinkers began to ask for it by name. Bourbon. Ironically, the county is dry today, just like Moore County in Tennessee, where Jack Daniel's is made. The finest whiskey comes out of the counties just to the west, around Lawrenceburg and in particular Bardstown, a quaint hamlet not far from the Mason-Dixon Line.

If you stroll through Bardstown today, you can just barely smell the stink of grain fermenting as you pass by Toddy's liquor shop, which has one of the finest collections of bourbons in the world, and a host of stores selling all manner of worthless souvenirs to tourists. As you near the end of town, there's a large stately brick house right on Third Street, where one Jim Beam lived, and where Beam's grandson Booker Noe lives today.

"He wasn't any old blowhard like me," says Booker about his grandfather, as we roll down the Bluegrass Highway toward Wild Turkey. "He was a quiet type of guy, debonair. He always wore a suit and tie, even when he went fishing."

James "Jim" Beauregard Beam was sixteen when he first started making whiskey, under the tutelage of his father, David. The business was called the Clear Springs Distillery Company, and it was located down the road from where the main Jim Beam distillery is today. After fourteen years of training on the job, Jim took over in 1894—the fourth generation of Beams to run a still. The bottle of Beam White Label today says, SAME RECIPE SINCE 1795, in reference to a recipe devised by Jacob, Jim's granddad, the first Beam to make whiskey in Kentucky.

Before Prohibition, the family distilled two brands of bourbon: Old Tub and Double Ford. The bottles were round and had no labels. Back in the horse-and-buggy days, Beam sold the whiskey to saloons, where drunks and businessmen alike drank it, sometimes before killing each other. Beam had a partner up in Chicago, and a brother, Tom Beam, in the saloon business in Kentucky. The word on Old Tub and Double Ford spread.

"He was not a chemist, see, but he knew about culturing yeast," says Booker about his granddad. "He made the strain of yeast we use today. He didn't have a microscope. Nowadays they use test tubes and microscopes. And he didn't have a fridge either, so in the old days he kept the yeast in a well, ya see. Groundwater is about 56 degrees

Booker Noe, T. Jeremiah Beam, Carl Beam, in the 1960s. *(Photo courtesy of Jim Beam Brands Co.)*

Fahrenheit all year round. So he hung it down there on a rope." Apparently, Beam held his yeast in such esteem he kept some of it in his house just in case something happened to his other stashes. Visitors noticed the unique odor of the stuff when they walked through the door.

Beam also kept ledgers recording sales, which show that business was pretty good in those days. The burgeoning steamship and railroad industries made commerce easier, so the whiskey started showing up in saloons farther and farther west. You'll notice that, in all the classic Western films, cowboys are drinking a brown liquid. Bourbon was the choice—and sometimes only—liquor available in the Wild West (unless you were tough, and perhaps dumb enough to land way down in tequila country). A lot of it was Beam's bourbon.

There were some fifty other working distilleries in Kentucky before Prohibition—all of them booming, clouds of dark coal smoke from the stills billowing into the sky. Then, on October 28, 1919, the United States government put out the fire. The days of moonshiners, smugglers, and Al Capone had arrived.

By the time the government passed the Volstead Act, otherwise known as the National Prohibition Act, Jim Beam was fifty-six years old. He'd done little outside of the liquor business his entire life. But government agents were starting to comb the Kentucky countryside, carrying guns and wearing their game faces. A very few distilleries were allowed to continue operation to make "medicinal whiskey," but Beam's wasn't one of them.

"I don't want to end up in that penitentiary," he told his family.

As grandson Booker points out, *"Goddamn it! Outlawing alcohol was the dumbest thing the government ever did. People aren't gonna do without their toddies! Their pick-me-ups! Hell."* Of that, there was no doubt. Jim Beam was able to sell his distillery pretty quickly to some "people who didn't mind getting their hands dirty and doing it illicitly," according to Booker. "A lot of them ended up in prison."

During Prohibition, an underground liquor industry thrived in Kentucky. Because the stills shot columns of telltale smoke up in the air, the guys running them had to operate at night (thus the term "moonshiner"). The hooch had to go straight from the still to the middle man. It couldn't be aged and darkened in charred oak barrels, where the cops would find it. So it was drunk clear and raw. It was called "white lightning" or "white dog" (because it had a nasty bite) or, as one witty writer recently joked, "Kentucky sushi."

A lot of the liquor went up north to Chicago, where one Al Capone was making more than $60,000 a year selling the stuff, quite a bit of money at the time. Gang warfare escalated over liquor turf, culminating in the infamous St. Valentine's Day Massacre in Chicago in 1929, when Capone's thugs shot seven of rival gang leader "Bugs" Moran's men dead.

"In its practical effects," says Andrew Sinclair in his book *Prohibition: The Era of Excess,* "national prohibition transferred $2 billion a year from the hands of brewers, distillers, and shareholders to the hands of murderers, crooks, and illiterates."

Meanwhile, Jim Beam was making a successful living. He invested in a coal mine in the mountains of western Kentucky, a rock quarry around the corner from the old Beam distillery, and some citrus groves in Florida. Wearing his trademark black three-piece suit and tie, white shirt, round spectacles, and pocket watch, he guarded his mines with the shotgun he'd eventually pass on to his grandson. He went on frequent fishing trips in Canada. He worked on his house, a redbrick building on the edge of Bardstown, which he purchased from the Bardstown Girls' Academy. All was well, but the taste for making whiskey never left him.

In the 1932 presidential election, the Democrats ran on a platform aiming to abolish the Prohibition Act, with a candidate who would go on to serve four terms—Franklin Delano Roosevelt (who preferred a Dirty Martini by the way). FDR was no fool. Naturally, he won, and on December 5, 1933, the federal government repealed the Eighteenth Amendment.

On December 7, just two days later, Jim Beam—now seventy years old—applied for a new distilling license and was assigned DSP License Number 230, the same one he'd had before Prohibition. With the help of his son Jeremiah, fresh out of the University of Kentucky, Beam rebuilt the distillery in one hundred twenty days in Clermont, where the company's main facility is today. Rather than Old Tub or Double Ford, as the Beam whiskey was called before, he decided to name the new liquor Jim Beam Kentucky Straight Bourbon.

If there was any good news for the whiskey business to come out of Prohibition, it was the fact that drinking on the sly made it impossible to get off on beer and wine. You had to go for the greater bang per ounce so you could get drunk on whatever could fit in a flask concealed in your pocket. Whiskey and gin emerged as the drinks of choice when Prohibition was repealed.

The name aside, Jim Beam's new whiskey wasn't any different from the old stuff: a liquor made from very specific amounts of corn, barley, and rye, aged four years in new charred oak barrels. Beam created a fresh white label with his name on it. Competition was tough; the flood of Canadian whiskey over the border during and after Prohibition made things hard on American distillers at first. Whiskey had to be aged before it could hit the market, but in Canada reserves were ready to go. (See Seagram's: A Dynasty Founded on Rumrunning later in the book.) Still, Beam's booze was a hit in no time, and it was quickly on its way to becoming the bestselling bourbon in the world.

"He worked all the time," remembers Booker. "Whiskey was what he knew. He made good whiskey and people loved it." Just a teenager back then, Booker began spending more time with his grandfather—going fishing, strolling around the distillery, cruising in the old man's 1939 Cadillac Coupe. "He was known to have a highball sometimes," Booker says, "but honest to God, I never once saw him take a drink. He didn't set around like me and drink. I drink at the drop of a hat. *Hey, you're not going to print that are ya?* Aw, shit. I don't give a damn what ya write. Hell."

Jim Beam died in December 1947, at his home in Bardstown, quite possibly at the hands of his grandson, Booker, who'd delivered him some birds to eat two days earlier on Christmas Day. "He made it to eighty-three, which is pretty good, especially in those days," Booker notes. "He got baptized three months before, so if he'd done any sinning in his life, it all disappeared before he died." Four years later, in August 1951, Booker, then twenty-one years old, joined the company.

By that time, Jim Beam's son, Jeremiah, was running the show. The whiskey was all handmade, "stirred with a stick." A decade later, Booker became master distiller. Over the next forty years, a Rube Goldberg–style assembly line would take the place of the factory's old-fashioned innards, and production would increase by twelve times. "When I started we made forty thousand gallons a week," says Booker. "Now we make *eighty thousand gallons a day*. We use the same grain, the same yeast, the same everything. But it's all automated."

Today, Booker's son, Freddy, is running the business side, while one Jerry Dalton has become the master distiller, the first non-Beam to hold the title. Under their command, the company filled its nine millionth barrel of whiskey in July 2002, the tally counting only liquor made since Jim Beam incorporated after Prohibition. That comes out to be, oh, 280 million cases of bourbon, or 115 billion drinks.

As we are driving home from the Wild Turkey distillery after the Bourbon Hall of Fame party, one of those nasty Kentucky rainstorms sweeps over the highway. In the passenger's-side front seat, Booker rolls his eyes and stares out the windshield, which looks like it's been coated with Vaseline. In the backseat, a trophy copper still with a black plaque honoring Jim Beam's induction to the Hall of Fame sits next to Booker's gray fedora.

"*Whoa!*" Booker yells, the rain blinding us. "*You watch that road, Jim! You put on your brakes on that goddamn slick highway . . . oh, hell. Damn!*"

"I got it," says Jim, white knuckling the wheel, his eyes straining to catch a glimpse of the double yellow line.

"*Goddamn!*" Booker says again. "Now where was I?" He was talking about how much he likes drinking his own brand of bourbon—Booker's—and about his diabetes. Aren't people who have blood sugar problems like diabetes supposed to lay off the booze? "*Hell no!*" he says. "If I stayed plastered all the time, I'd be fine. But the liver can't handle it. Are you quoting me? Aw, hell, I don't give a shit. I have a toddy every day. *Several!* It levels off the sugar in your blood. Ask any doctor." By the way, he's dead wrong.

JIM BEAM'S SMALL BATCH BOURBONS

School days were all about drinking White Label shots with beer chasers. And for folks who manage to graduate . . .

🥃 **BAKER'S:** A deep amber whiskey with hints of fruit, caramel, and nut, this bourbon is generally a hit among folks who like cognac. (Baker's happens to be my favorite bourbon in the world, if that counts for anything.) It's made from an old family recipe preferred by Jim Beam's grandnephew, Baker Beam, using an old strain of jug yeast that's been in the family for decades. The whiskey is aged seven years and comes dressed up in a slope-shoulder wine bottle.

🥃 **BASIL HAYDEN:** This delicious whiskey's named after an eighteenth-century master distiller. Basil Hayden grew up in Maryland, where he learned to make rye. When he moved to Kentucky in 1796, Hayden added corn to the recipe, the same recipe the Jim Beam distillery uses to produce the bottle that now bears his name. The mash contains twice as much rye as most other bourbons, and you can taste it. Aged eight years and bottled at 80 proof, Basil Hayden is light and mellow on the tongue—great for breakfast or first-time drinkers.

So when Booker pours a tall one, does he like to drink, say, Wild Turkey? Maker's Mark?

"Don't ask me no dumb-ass questions. I drink Booker's bourbon, with water. Booker's has the most body. It has the most flavor."

Back in 1987, the old man launched his own "small batch" bourbon, bottled under his own name. To produce the stuff, he personally samples barrels of the finest whiskey from what he calls the "center cut" of the rack house, bourbon aged six to eight years. Booker's is sold in a wine bottle, available in varying strengths depending on the batch, from 121 to 127 proof. In other words, it mixes well with a dash of water. Booker himself is a walking advertisement.

"As far as I know, it's the only uncut, unfiltered, unadulterated bourbon in the world—straight from the barrel. *Goddamn right!* That's the way it was one hundred fifty years ago, and that's the way I like it."

As we pull up into Bardstown, the rain stops and the sun cuts through the clouds. Jim pulls around a corner and into the driveway of a redbrick house with a large front lawn and a circular blossoming flower bed. Welcome to the original Jim Beam's house, at one time the Bardstown Girls' Academy, now the home of Jim Beam Brands master distiller emeritus Booker Noe. The home is a big but modest

KNOB CREEK: This drink's named after Abraham Lincoln's childhood home in Kentucky. The best known of all small batch bourbons these days, Knob Creek spends nine years "getting to know the inside of a new charred American white oak barrel," as the Beam folks like to put it. The barrels are charred up to "level four," meaning they're burned pretty good. The dark caramelized wood gives the whiskey its signature earthy aroma, delicate sweetness, and dark amber color. It's bottled at 100 proof, like most good bourbons were way back when.

BOOKER'S: For years, Beam master distiller emeritus Booker Noe used to bottle a bourbon straight from the barrel at Christmastime for his friends—uncut, unfiltered, untouched. The stuff became a hit among in-the-know locals. So in 1988, he decided to brand and market it (Booker's True Barrel Bourbon). This liquor goes down like a hot mystery novel—hints and clues of flavors (oak, tobacco, vanilla), legs that coat a glass like fishnet, and a long, hot finish. At proofs that vary from barrel to barrel (121–127 proof), Booker's comes with a Joe Frazier–style right hook packed inside each bottle.

place, a classic old suburban beauty with a couple added touches out back—a smokehouse for ham and a makeshift pond where Booker keeps bluegill for eating. (The pond looks like a giant hot tub that hasn't been cleaned in, well, ever.) His son, Freddy, lives right next door.

Booker climbs out of the minivan and slams the door shut behind him. Without looking back, he waves his hand in the air and says with a deep Southern drawl, *"Allll right."* Then he opens the door to his house and disappears inside, where his Jack Russell terrier, Spot, is waiting, and no doubt a toddy of Booker's bourbon as well.

THE MINT JULEP

The julep is probably as old as alcohol itself, perhaps even older. The Arabs called it *julab*. The Persians called it *gulab*. Technically, it means rose water, and it came to denote any liquid infused with the essence of something else. Here in the States, julep generally means bourbon flavored with sugar and mint. And make sure you get the mixology right, lest you wind up on the business end of a double barrel.

As the prevailing legend has it, the origin of the Mint Julep goes something like this: One day, a transient on the Mississippi came ashore hunting for some springwater to dilute a stiff batch of whiskey. Finding some wild mint growing on the riverbank, he tossed a bunch in. That's pretty much the story, with the noted exception of a dash of sugar, which was added later. Way back in 1820, the *Old American Encyclopedia* described drinking in the South: "A fashion at the South was to take a glass of whiskey, flavored with mint, soon after waking; and so conducive to health was this nostrum esteemed that no sex, and scarcely any age, were deemed exempt from its application."

Today, the Mint Julep is a staple drink all over the South. It's also the official drink of the Kentucky Derby. The following recipe is my favorite, culled from a variety of sources in Bardstown and Louisville, Kentucky. It'll take twenty-four hours, so plan accordingly.

- Make a batch of simple syrup. Throw a cup of plain granulated white sugar and a cup of freshwater (springwater if possible) into a pot. Heat it until the sugar melts into the water, stirring occasionally. Then let it cool.

- Take a pile of fresh mint leaves without stems, about enough to make a loose ball the size of a large fist. Throw that in a big bowl with a cup of bourbon. Then muddle it up using any instrument you've got.

- Take a break for a couple hours. Ask yourself, what is life? Is there a God? Should socks always have to match, or is it okay to wear a blue one and a black one if you're sure that no one will notice?

- Take the rest of the bottle of bourbon and dump it in the bowl, along with about a cup to a cup and a half of your cooled syrup. (However you like—taste it as you go.) Stir the concoction; then put it in the refrigerator overnight.

- Wake up the next day. Put tall cocktail glasses in the freezer to chill. Then invite some friends over.

- When ready, fill your chilled cocktail glasses with crushed ice (snobby Southern folk will require silver cups). Stir up your Mint Julep, and start pouring. Garnish with a mint sprig, and raise a toast.

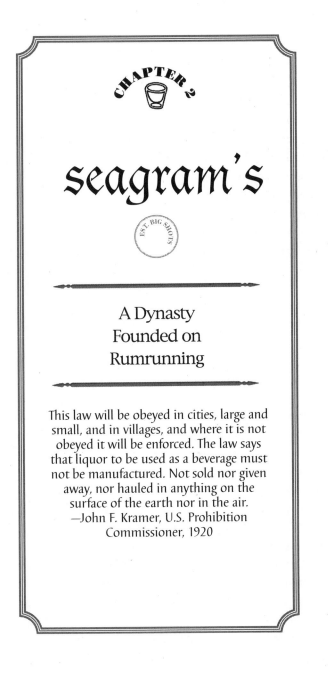

CHAPTER 2

seagram's

EST. BIG SHOTS

A Dynasty
Founded on
Rumrunning

This law will be obeyed in cities, large and
small, and in villages, and where it is not
obeyed it will be enforced. The law says
that liquor to be used as a beverage must
not be manufactured. Not sold nor given
away, nor hauled in anything on the
surface of the earth nor in the air.
—John F. Kramer, U.S. Prohibition
Commissioner, 1920

etween the years 1920 and 1930—the heyday of the Prohibition era—some thirty-four thousand Americans drank themselves to death. Two thousand gangsters and five hundred federal
agents were murdered as a result of the illicit booze frenzy. The government seized more than a billion gallons of liquor during this country's "noble experiment."

"Good old Prohibition days," as the drunk tank nurse says in Billy
Wilder's classic 1945 film, *The Lost Weekend*. "You should've seen the
[drunk tank] then. This is nothing. Back then we really had a turnover.
Standing room only."

Now one has to wonder where all this booze was coming from.
The answer is everywhere. It was made overseas and sold in America
as "medicine" (Laphroaig Scotch, for example), whipped up in makeshift distilleries in the South, brewed crudely in bathtubs all over the
forty-eight states.

Perhaps no one was making more money off the illicit liquor trade
during Prohibition than a couple of brothers, Harry and Samuel Bronfman, the sons of Orthodox Jewish Russian immigrants living in Canada.
The brothers got their start in the liquor trade selling whiskey out of
the hotels they owned in Saskatchewan about 150 miles north of the
U.S. border. They made poor-quality hooch with counterfeit Scotch
whiskey labels and sold it to thirsty smugglers, who could make a fast
buck by driving a fast car into American territory.

In Canada at the time, making liquor was perfectly legal. Running it
over the border was not. The Bronfmans used the laws against liquor
in their favor by making it easy for other people to break these laws.
Then they sat back and skimmed the foam off the top. And there was
nothing anybody could do about it. As one Bronfman biographer, Peter C. Newman, in his book *King of the Castle*, put it: "Sometimes it almost seemed that the American Congress and the Canadian federal
and provincial legislatures must have secretly held a grand conclave to
decide one issue: how they could draft antiliquor laws and regulations
that would help maximize the Bronfman brothers' bootlegging profits."

By 1928, the Bronfmans had made enough cash to invest in a big-
time legitimate liquor operation. So they bought a distillery—a small

company called Joseph E. Seagram and Sons, Limited—and took the Seagram name for their own, slapping it across their stationery and their liquor bottles. Within just a few years, the family would become the largest producer of spirits in the world. They would become one of the richest families in the history of the planet—the "Rothschilds of the West," a Jewish dynasty to rival any. ("Bronfman," it's worth noting, means "whiskey man" in Yiddish. You can't *make* this stuff up.)

How much power did this family wield? By the 1970s, the Bronfmans had amassed a fortune of $7 billion and a staggering catalog of liquors, which included not just Seagram's Crown Seven, VO, and Seagram's Gin, but brands like Crown Royal, Chivas Regal, The Glenlivet, White Horse, Gordon's Gin and Vodka, Jameson Irish Whiskey, Captain Morgan and Myer's rums, not to mention hundreds of wine labels from France, Italy, Denmark, Germany, and Puerto Rico. Who knew they made wine in Puerto Rico? The Bronfmans did.

Today, the Bronfmans are in the news again in a big way. But this time, the story's not about the compounding of extraordinary wealth and power, but the squandering of it. Edgar Jr., the family's swarthy scion, who's overseen the company since 1994, began moving the family interests away from the bread-and-butter booze industry into Hollywood during the tech boom. In his younger years, Bronfman had tested the waters as a film producer (*The Border*, 1982, starring Jack Nicholson), and as a music lyricist ("I want to hold your body next to mine / I want to hurry love and take my time"). As CEO of Seagram's, he purchased 80 percent of MCA, parent company of Universal Studios and a collection of music and television operations, for $5.7 billion. In 2000, Edgar Jr. made a deal with a French company called Vivendi, in essence selling his company in hopes of amalgamating a global media empire that could rival big guys like Time Warner and Disney.

In a couple years' time, the Bronfmans would see *$3.5 billion* of their fortune evaporate into thin air as a result of the deal. Vivendi would post a $25.6 billion loss in 2002—*the largest single-year loss ever in French corporate history.* The "angel's share"? Yeah, right. It was a "disaster," in Edgar Jr.'s own words. The poor guy was hung out to dry. *New York* magazine called him "possibly the stupidest person in the media business."

And so it goes, the trials and tribulations of the Rothschilds of the West. Even now, eighty years after the Bronfmans first started in the liquor business, the details of the family operations are still shocking—and entertaining—to say the least. If Edgar Jr. wanted to make a big earner while running Universal Studios, one wonders why he didn't make a film about his own family. The plot would go something like this . . .

Seagram's—the King of Canadian Whiskey—first became popular in the States under the stewardship of Joseph Seagram back in the 1880s, a few decades before the Bronfmans would purchase the label. At the time, Canadian whiskey was "straight" whiskey. Northern distillers had yet to adopt whiskey blending, which was all the rage in Scotland, thanks to labels like Johnnie Walker, Chivas, and Teacher's. Joseph Seagram was one of the first Canadian producers to make a blended whiskey.

He called his whiskey Seagram's 83, to celebrate the year he'd founded the Joseph Seagram Flour Mill and Distillery Company, based in Waterloo, Ontario, forty miles west of Toronto. He concentrated heavily on the export market in the U.S. and in Europe. In Canada, distillers used a much higher concentration of rye to make whiskey, so it has a distinctive flavor when compared to American whiskies, which are made with a higher percentage of corn and are thus sweeter and darker. By 1911, Seagram's 83 was the most popular Canadian whiskey in the States. That year, the company launched another brand—Seagram's VO—to celebrate the marriage of Joseph Seagram's son, Thomas. The name came up over a dinner conversation. VO stands for "Very Own" (it was the family's reserve blend) rather than "Very Old," as the cognac parlance goes.

Joseph Seagram died in 1919. Perhaps the news that booze was going to be outlawed in the U.S. was enough to kill him. After his death, the Seagram company went public. It was the whiskey's quality and the Seagram name that first drew the thirsty eye of Samuel and Harry Bronfman.

The Bronfman brothers were the sons of immigrants who'd left Russia in the 1880s to escape the bloody pogroms. They'd landed in a pioneer settlement in eastern Saskatchewan—rugged, unforgiving territory. The family patriarch, an Orthodox Jew named Ekiel, eked out a living trading horses.

Ekiel's horse-trading deals often went down in bars the old-fashioned way—over a drink and a handshake. According to family legend, young Samuel Bronfman once accompanied his father to the bar at a place called the Langham Hotel to watch Dad make a deal. Afterward, he looked up and said, "The Langham's bar makes more profit than we do, Father. Instead of selling horses, we should be selling drinks." Smart kid.

When old enough, the Bronfman brothers went into the hotel business and started selling drinks. A lot of them. Right from the start, their clientele was of dubious character. The hotels—places like the Balmoral in Yorkton, Saskatchewan, and the Anglo American in Emerson, Manitoba—benefited from the railways that were slowly snaking across Canada around the turn of the twentieth century. Workmen and traveling salesmen would come in looking for a meal, a drink, and some companionship. *Female* companionship. When Samuel Bronfman was questioned later in life about whether he ran glorified brothels in his youth, he would answer: "If they were, then they were the best in the West!"

The Bronfmans' saga might be the greatest right-place-right-time story in history. When Prohibition began in the States, the demand for Canadian whiskey exploded. If you lived near the border, heading over it for a booze run was far easier than making the stuff yourself. Readers of the daily papers were consumed with exotic tales of amateur booze runs gone wrong. Smugglers ran booze over the border hidden in soda bottles, in jars of every kind of food imaginable, inside eggshells, in bottles strapped beneath the bodies of cars. Runners shipped loads in boats over the Great Lakes, having paid customs officials extra on the Canadian side after claiming the cargo was headed to ports like Havana, where liquor was legal. At one point in 1929, a media frenzy erupted after a customs official killed a man at the border because he mistakenly thought the man was transporting liquor. The innocent man was shot dead right in his car, his wife and two lads sitting next to him.

Still, the cash-only business continued. Clearly there was a demand for a well-lubricated liquor smuggling operation. Any group who could pull it off on a mass scale would be in a position to corner the market.

Recognizing the bundle of cash to be made, the Bronfmans purchased crude distilling equipment from the Brewers' and Bottlers' Supplies Company in Winnipeg, and started making 65 proof white grain spirit at a facility in Yorkton, Saskatchewan. They then added some Scotch whiskey and a little burned sugar for color. Voilà: Scotch whiskey. They hired a local firm to produce labels for them.

According to biographer Peter C. Newman, they poured all the hooch out of one big vat and slapped different counterfeit labels on the bottles. Johnny Walker, for example (as opposed to Johnnie Walker) went for $45 a case. Glen Levitt (after The Glenlivet, a Scotch brand the company would later own) went for a little more.

While brother Harry managed the production, Sam traveled through the U.S. to make connections with bootleggers and illegal importers. (This foreshadowed the split in the family later; part of the burgeoning empire would stay in Canada while the more powerful part would move to New York. Today, you can purchase Seagram's VO, which is a Canadian whiskey, and Seagram's Crown Seven, which is American corn whiskey.)

In no time, the Bronfmans' operation was up and rolling. Harry started a shipping company called the Trans-Canada Transportation Limited. Smugglers could then slip over the border more easily by flashing work papers at customs officials. The ride was a good 150 miles from the border, through rural Saskatchewan. The smugglers' automobile of choice was called the Studebaker "Whiskey Six." As Newman described the car in *King of the Castle*:

> Fully stripped down, with reinforced springs and upholstery removed, it could carry forty cases of whisky, worth $2,000. In case he might be missing some business, Harry [Bronfman] opened up the City Garage next to his booze palace in Yorkton so that the American bootleggers could get their automobiles serviced while they were waiting for a new load. He also kept a stock of used cars, filled with booze, in the front of his hotel and sold them "as is" to adventurous Saskatchewan farmers anxious to engage in a little moonlighting.

To make the smuggler's job even easier, the brothers later opened "satellite warehouses" closer to the border, some of them less than a dozen miles from U.S. territory. In Canada, none of this activity was illegal. It was all straight up, as far as the Bronfmans were concerned. And there was nothing the law could do about it. The boys also started importing legitimate Scotch whiskey from across the pond around this time—Dewar's, Black & White, Johnnie Walker. By 1922, they were controlling the booze industry in all of midwestern Canada.

Cash was rolling in by the barrel. But there were changes looming over the border. The Bronfmans knew that Prohibition wouldn't last forever, and in order to keep their business healthy and their customers loaded, they'd have to go legit. The market over the border would someday open up like a raw wound, and the Bronfmans were poising themselves to clean it out with pure 86 proof Canadian whiskey.

In 1924, the Bronfmans opened a large distillery in Ville La Salle outside Montreal and started pumping out liquor. They named their company Distillers Corporation Limited. Four years later, they purchased the Seagram distillery, married the two companies, and went public—250,000 shares at $15 a shot—while maintaining a majority ownership. Seagram's as we know it was born.

The local market proved lucrative. But the Bronfmans were really interested in the States. Distilleries all over America had been closed and padlocked since 1919, and good whiskey takes years to make, with the aging process and all. In contrast, the Bronfmans had a huge stock of aging mellowed whiskey ready to roll.

On December 5, 1933, the Eighteenth Amendment was repealed. The Bronfmans invaded the States. For sale in stores nationwide: Seagram's VO, Seagram's 83, Seagram's Gin, Seagram's Bourbon, and Seagram's Rye. American liquor companies couldn't possibly keep up. Thirsty boozers guzzled the Bronfmans' liquor and stumbled gleefully back to the store to buy more.

Within sixty days of the end of Prohibition, as Sam Bronfman would later say, "We were able to tell the public that the Seagram whiskeys were outselling all others throughout the country." In less than two years, the company was selling more than a million cases annually, leading the U.S. in distilled spirit sales.

Having conquered the American market, the Bronfmans then decided to move in the ground troops. They bought out the Rossville Union Distillery in Lawrenceburg, Indiana, and the Calvert distillery in Relay, Maryland. "Mr. Sam," as he became known to his employees, began importing aged casks of Canadian whiskey into the States and blending it with the American stuff. He opened new headquarters at the shiny Chrysler building in the financial capital of the world—Midtown Manhattan—in October 1934.

Mr. Sam was ready to launch some new brands. He would oversee the blending of these new whiskies himself. ("Distilling is a science," he was known to say. "Blending is an art.") These liquors, he assured his colleagues, would conquer the world.

THE WIDE WORLD OF WHISKEY

The Irish say they invented whiskey. The Scots say they did. One thing's for sure: the Canadians and Americans did *not*, though both have added their distinctive touches to the art. And never mind Japan and India. Though they make good whiskey over there (try Suntory from Japan), the stuff isn't widely available in the States. So what gives each whiskey its unique flavor?

CANADIAN: According to Canadian law, the whiskey produced in that country has to be 90 proof or lighter, must be aged at least three years, and must be distilled from grain. Most Canadian distillers use a much higher content of rye, with smaller percentages of corn and barley. The flavor is less sweet and perhaps a touch more sour, with a lighter body and color. These whiskies are blended (not single malts), and damn it, they taste good. Because of the colder climate, more like that of Scotland than that of Kentucky, Canadian whiskey ages more slowly. Bestsellers in the States: Crown Royal, followed by Seagram's VO.

AMERICAN: Of the four, American whiskies tend to be sweeter because of the corn used. The traditional distilling method that arose out of Kentucky, Tennessee, Maryland, Virginia, Pennsylvania, and Indiana involves a high percentage of corn, 51 percent or more by law, though sometimes as much as three-quarters. The rest is mostly rye and barley and sometimes wheat. Down south, where it's hot in the summer and cold in the winter, the whiskies expand and contract in the changing climate, so they have more interaction with the wood they're aged in. They age more quickly as a result. Bestsellers in the States: Jack Daniel's (Tennessee sour mash whiskey), followed by Jim Beam (bourbon).

As then–company vice president Frank Schwengel later remembered:

There was a period of several months during 1934 when we had daily sessions, sometimes lasting far into the night. We'd try twelve, fifteen, sometimes two dozen samples. They were numbered consecutively and nobody knew what was in the blend. Finally, we all agreed on sample number seven, and someone said, "Well, you can't just call it number seven. . . . " Mr. Sam suggested adding the word "crown," meaning that this was to be the crowning product in the history of Seagram.

SCOTCH: Scotland's whiskies are made of the "ménage à trois" of barley, yeast, and water. Much of the barley is malted, meaning it's soaked in water, then left out to germinate. The barley is then cooked and/or dried over peat fire, which gives Scotch whiskey its familiar smoky taste. Peat is basically decomposed vegetable matter harvested all over Scotland. The island distilleries, such as Laphroaig, Lagavulin, and Bowmore, use peat that's been scented by sea winds, thus the salt and seaweed hints you find in their flavors. Today, most of the whiskies from Scotland are blends of single malts (the most popular blends in the States are Dewar's, followed by Johnnie Walker Red and then Black), while a small percentage of higher-priced whiskies are single malts (The Glenlivet is the most popular in the U.S., followed by Glenfiddich).

IRISH: As far as ingredients go, the whiskey from Ireland is very similar to that of neighboring Scotland. The difference in flavor is huge. Why? Unlike the Scots, the Irish dry their malted barley in closed kilns, rather than over peat fires. So you don't get that smoky peat flavor. Instead, you get a flavor closer to the cereals themselves—pure barley malt, with color and richness sucked out of the oak barrels the whiskey is aged in. Also, the Irish usually triple distill and blend their whiskies (the case with Jameson, for example, the most popular Irish whiskey in the States), so you get a lighter flavor. Are there Irish single malts? You bet. Try the old standard, Bushmills ten-year-old Single Malt Irish Whiskey, out of Northern Ireland.

In 1934, happy drinkers were introduced to three new American whiskeys: Seagram Crown, Seagram Five Crown, and Seagram Seven Crown. Within a decade, two would bite the dust in favor of Seven Crown, a blend of whiskies aged at least four years, made from corn, rye, and barley grown in the Midwest. The liquor was aged in new and used charred white oak barrels. Few would call Seven Crown great whiskey by today's standards. But there was nothing on the market at a comparable price that could match it at the time.

In 1939, the Bronfmans also launched Crown Royal, a blended Canadian whiskey, created in honor of George VI and Queen Elizabeth's visit to Canada that year. Crown Royal is today the bestselling Canadian whiskey in America.

Once World War II started and alcohol production in the States was restricted by the government, the Bronfmans began investing in overseas ventures, especially rum distilleries in the Caribbean. The firm would later buy Captain Morgan's Original rum in 1983 (today, the second-largest rum brand behind Bacardi). They also bought the Chivas Regal label in Scotland for a mere £80,000. Mr. Sam pushed the Chivas brand particularly hard as the Rolls-Royce of Scotch whiskies. But it was good old Crown Seven that would lead the company's portfolio.

In 1946, the Seagram company sold 2.5 million cases of Crown Seven. A year later, they sold 4.5 million cases. By 1948, the number hit eight million. It was the undisputed heavyweight champion, the Joe Louis of whiskies, packing that KO punch that hit the spot if you were a drunk or an insomniac. In those days, a good dinner was a steak and a Seagram's whiskey, unless you were a Martini man or you'd traveled to Europe and knew the lure of a good Scotch or cognac.

The Bronfmans' company was growing at an astonishing rate, adding liquor brand after liquor brand to the portfolio. The brothers were quickly becoming two of the richest men in the world. By the end of the 1950s, Samuel Bronfman—who was by then leading the company—was paying himself $351,042 a year, back then a phenomenal sum. He was a short man, five foot and change, with a little meat-and-potatoes gut and a head of thinning hair. But he was an intimidator—tough, little, Jewish. Like other moguls of the time, he began to indulge himself.

To house the company's headquarters, the Bronfman clan hired famed architect Ludwig Mies van der Rohe to build a Seagram's tower in Manhattan. The Seagram Building opened in 1958—a trendsetter in high-rise urban architecture, thirty-eight glorious shimmering stories right on Park Avenue. Next, the Bronfmans started shopping around for a few things to hang on the walls. They began investing in what would become one of the most remarkable art collections in the world, with works by Picasso, Joan Miró, Rodin, Alfred Stieglitz, Mark Rothko, and any number of other major artists. The collection alone would be worth over $15 million by the century's end.

Right around the time the Seagram Building opened, the cocktail craze was taking hold of America. Bartenders all over the country were whipping up Vodkatinis and Moscow Mules as quickly as their hands could move. Most of the drinks called for clear spirits like gin and vodka. Luckily, Seagram's had money invested in both. And in

1965, the company kicked off a series of ads promoting what has since become one of the world's most popular cocktails—7&7—Seagram's own American blended whiskey over ice with 7 Up. If you're in a nice joint, the barman might throw in a lime. A year later, the company would ship their 150 millionth case of Seven Crown.

In 1971, Mr. Sam died. But the Seagram's empire didn't. Edgar Bronfman Sr. took over, and during his reign, the company thrived. Edgar Sr. was president of the World Jewish Congress, a fearless political mogul who, with the aid of his high-powered cronies, was responsible for, among other things, outing former United Nations secretary general Kurt Waldheim as a onetime Nazi. Edgar Sr. could handle himself in business as well. By the end of the seventies, he owned or marketed five bourbons, seven blended American whiskies, twenty-five Canadian whiskies, five Irish whiskies (including Jameson *and* Bushmills), sixteen Scotches (Chivas, Glenlivet, White Horse), fourteen gins, twelve vodkas, thirty-one rums, and four tequila brands. The company's signature Seven Crown and VO were the numbers one and two whiskey brands in the world. This, not to mention dozens of liqueurs, vermouths, and cognacs, cocktail mixes, and 358 wine, sherry, and port labels. The company also owned oil and real estate interests in twenty-three states and the District of Columbia.

During his twenty-three years as CEO, Edgar Sr. watched the company's sales rise from $1.5 billion to $5.2 billion. But he would retire too, leaving the reins of this massive conglomerate to a third generation of Bronfmans. It was Edgar Jr.'s turn, and this made a lot of people very, very nervous. Even Mr. Sam himself was quoted way back in 1966 (when Edgar Jr. was just eleven years old) expressing doubt about the family's future.

"You've heard about shirtsleeves to shirtsleeves in three generations," Mr. Sam had told *Fortune* magazine in 1966. "I'm worried about the third generation. Empires have come and gone."

Edgar Jr. first took the reins of Seagram's in 1994, amid a swirl of press over whether he was the right man for the job. Edgar Jr. had skipped college, eloped with an actress, done everything that a rebellious rich kid is supposed to do. The question was, could he run a company the size of Seagram's?

A dark-skinned man with brown hair combed back, a prominent nose, and a penchant for facial scruff, Edgar Jr. sported the Hollywood-executive look. During the gravy years of the bull market, alcohol consumption was on the decline in the States, so the new CEO started moving investments into the entertainment business. Edgar Jr. bought up MCA (which owned Universal Studios), plus a couple big-time record labels—in particular, Polygram NV, the world's largest label, for $10.4 billion. Instead of focusing on whiskey and gin, the Bronfmans were now selling Snoop Dogg albums. ("Now that I got me some Seagram's gin / Everybody got they cups, but they ain't chipped in.")

From 1995 to 2000, Seagram stock appreciated 71 percent. But then again, everyone's stock was going through the roof during those years. Was Edgar Jr. a shrewd financial wizard, or was he just a flashy rich kid? The world was soon to find out.

On June 20, 2000, Edgar Jr. stood proudly with Jean-Marie Messier, the clownish-looking CEO of Vivendi—a French TV, Internet, and wireless communications firm—at a press conference in Paris to announce the merger of the two companies. Both men beamed as if they'd just won the lottery and they were announcing their good fortune to the world.

Vivendi had purchased Seagram's for $34 billion, they explained. To save the Bronfmans from tax burdens, Edgar Jr. had accepted payment in Vivendi stock. A colossal mistake.

Soon after, the Bronfman clan watched helplessly as Jean-Marie Messier began to make a series of bizarre financial deals that didn't quite square on the books. Messier was a player, but not a good one. When tensions arose between the two honchos, Messier lashed out, shocking the global business community.

"I think Edgar feels better being number two than number one," Messier was quoted saying. "He is free to say anything, knowing he doesn't make the final decision. So for me it's a perfect fit." Then, against the Bronfman clan's protestations, Messier took a favorite Mark Rothko painting from the Park Avenue Seagram Building and hung it in his New York apartment.

Meanwhile, reports began to surface that Vivendi's numbers didn't add up. Indeed, by October 2002, the company was $19 billion in debt. The stock dropped from $83.43 per share when the Seagram/Vivendi deal was made to $13.15. The Bronfmans were out $3.5 billion.

French and American investigators have since moved in, hunting for any legal wrongdoings. Jean-Marie Messier has been ousted. While the Bronfmans certainly aren't eating out of dog food cans, the loss was devastating. At press time for this book, Vivendi was selling off the famed Seagram art collection. "I'm heartbroken," Mr. Sam Bronfman's daughter, Phyllis Lambert, was quoted as saying in the *New York Times*. "This is part of a whole Greek tragedy."

Slapped with the task of picking up the pieces, Edgar Jr., now forty-eight years old, has been crucified by the media. And it has fallen to him to write the next chapter of this story, a weighty task to say the least. Unlike other power moguls who've been publicly humiliated in the last couple years, this one has one thing going for him: a liquor cabinet to rival any in the world.

CHAPTER 3

Jack Daniel's

EST. BIG SHOTS

A Classic American Whiskey, Distilled by a Nine Year Old

I can't help myself. I'm for anything
that gets you through the night, be it
prayer, tranquilizers, or a bottle of
Jack Daniel's.
—Frank Sinatra

In the summer of 1951, readers flipping through the July issue of *Fortune* magazine were treated to a mouthwatering story called "Rare Jack Daniel's." The article was about a tiny old-time distillery in the foothills of the Cumberland Mountains in Tennessee, where "the finest whiskey in the world" was made using an old family-held "secret." It was a story about a brand of whiskey that, in the early days of the Cold War, beat culture, and Mickey Mantle, scarce few had ever laid eyes on, let alone tasted. The first paragraph read as follows:

"If you've never heard of Jack Daniel's whiskey, so much the better. Its relative obscurity is part of its charm. For this backwoods brand of spirits, which is scarcely advertised at all and amounts to the merest ripple in the oceans of whiskey produced and consumed in the U.S., has become the beneficiary of a wonderful whispering campaign. Little knots of Jack Daniel fanatics are to be encountered in all parts of the country and in all walks of life. They pluck at one's sleeve and whisper, "Try some of this. It's made in a li'l ol' still way off somewhere in the hills of Tennessee. The same family has been making it by the same secret process for nearly a hundred years. It's expensive, and hard to get, but no other whiskey in the world tastes quite like it."

Has any liquor brand ever received such a blow job? ("Blow job" is a journalistic term, by the way, meaning a gratuitously generous story.) The *Fortune* piece featured photos of hillbillies dressed in baggy pants with suspenders and old saloon-style hats hanging around a distillery, staring bug-eyed into the camera's eye as if they'd never seen such a strange contraption in their lives. It was as if a new race of people rather than a whiskey had been discovered in the remote mountains of the South. That was 1951.

Less than two decades later, Jack Daniel's had turned into one of the most coveted brands of liquor in the world. It was *the* drink for lots of crowds by the 1960s. It carried the aura of masculinity, a strange dichotomy of youthful rebellion and aged worldliness.

The ever-drunken Nobel Prize winner William Faulkner: "It's a good thing that in a changing world there are some unchanging things you can count on, like the quality of Jack Daniel's."

Vice President John Nance Garner, who served under FDR, when he toasted Jack Daniel's: "Strike a blow for liberty!"

The man most responsible for the whiskey's postwar popularity was the boss of bosses, arguably the coolest cat ever to walk the planet. During World War II, Jackie Gleason introduced Frank Sinatra to Jack Daniel's. Thereafter, JD became the official drink of the Rat Pack, and Sinatra became known as "Jack's Original Test Pilot."

The crooner was dangerously particular about how he liked his JD. Three or four cubes. Two fingers of Jack. The rest water, in a rocks glass. And he drank right-handed. "*This* is a gentleman's drink," he'd say, if the bartender got it right. And if the bartender didn't, he was taken out into the alley and whacked by mobsters.

While I was growing up in suburban New Jersey in the seventies, my old man was a Bud drinker—a six-pack of cans a day on weekends. But when we went out to dinner, generally to a place called Pal's Cabin in West Orange, he would invariably greet the waiter with three words: "Jack Daniel's. Rocks." Steak and a couple Jacks—that's what a man ordered when he was wearing a tie.

Today the liquor's the bestselling American whiskey in the world. It's often associated with boozers who guzzle it in shots or with a mixer. Sixty percent of the stuff is drunk with Coke these days—a disgraceful error.

"The finest whiskey in the world," as *Fortune* called it, deserves to be sipped in a glass neat or with a dash of water or a couple cubes. Otherwise the "family secret" that Jack Daniel instilled in his famous whiskey during his lifetime is lost on the palate.

Jasper Newton "Jack" Daniel was most likely born in 1846, the tenth of thirteen children. (Never mind that his gravestone in Lynchburg, Tennessee, says that he was born in 1850. They didn't have fact checkers back then.) At the time, just as it is today, Lynchburg was a tiny speck of civilization tucked away in the hills, a long-ass ride from anywhere, population 361 according to the original Jack Daniel's whiskey label. The nearest cities—railroad towns Chattanooga and burgeoning Nashville—were some seventy miles in either direction, a brutal ride in the horse-and-buggy days.

When Jack was two, his mother died. A couple years later, his father, Calaway Daniel, remarried, and little Jack didn't take it lightly. With twelve brothers and sisters, he was a neglected kid. So he ran away—all the way to the neighbor's farm, where "Uncle Felix" (no relation) lived. A short time later, one of the tiny community's leaders took the boy in, giving the orphan a home (think Albert on *Little House on the Prairie*). The Reverend Dan Call was a Lutheran preacher who owned a general store and a still at a place called Louse Creek, and he needed an apprentice. Not only did Jack find a home— he found a trade as well.

At just nine years old, Jack Daniel began making whiskey.

That year, the "secret way" of making Jack Daniel's whiskey, "handed down from father to son," was actually handed down to Jack Daniel from an African-American slave. Brother Dan Call "owned" a man named Nearest Green, who taught the boy how to make whiskey the old Tennessee way.

At the time, there were seventeen other distilleries in Lynchburg and plenty more throughout the state. Lynchburg is on the edge of the same limestone shelf that lies beneath bourbon country in Kentucky, with similar crisp mineral-free water and fertile soil that's great for growing corn, barley, and rye.

Now Reverand Call had a problem. In the years before the Civil War, a maniacal temperance movement was brewing, led by fervent religious groups, mainly hysterical women. It started in the Northeast. (Maine was the first state to outlaw booze, in 1846.) It quickly spread like ringworm in a preschool. By the 1850s, congregationalists in Tennessee didn't take kindly to a preacher who made whiskey, so Brother Call found himself in a tough spot.

"The reverend's wife thought he should spend more time preaching than making whiskey," according to current Lynchburg resident and Jack Daniel's great-grandniece, Lynne Tolley, author of the *Jack Daniel's Cookbook*. "So he sold the business."

In 1863, at just thirteen years old, Jack Daniel took ownership of his first distillery, along with Brother Call's farm and his general store. Jack had been saving while working for the reverend. And Call gave him a good deal, because he had to unload the operation quickly to save his reputation. It was great timing, considering the fact that Union and Confederate troops were pouring into Tennessee as well as other states to beat the hell out of each other during what the South still calls "the War of Northern Aggression."

During the Civil War, the Yanks attacked Southern troops in the hills and hollows around Lynchburg, taking and retaking what is now Moore County seven times. The area was crawling with soldiers, the hills marked by smoke columns rising off bivouacs. The upheaval made it difficult for young Jack to maintain supplies of grain for the still, but he managed.

A smart businessman, and too young to go to war (perhaps too short also: he stood only five foot two fully grown), Daniel sold some of his first whiskey to the troops—on both sides.

One day when he was nineteen, while walking through a rugged ravine about a mile outside town, Jack Daniel stumbled across a cave on the banks of Mulberry Creek in the hills of Lynchburg. The cave, set at the base of a limestone cliff, was vomiting a steady stream of cool springwater, feeding a handful of thirsty sugar maples below. The water flowed at a constant 56 degrees Fahrenheit, fresh and chilly. Jack tasted it, and the saliva began to flow from his mouth. Tennessee gold. It was the perfect spot to set up a still.

Daniel bought Cave Spring Hollow and began building on the bank of Mulberry Creek. It was 1865, the year the Civil War ended, the year Abraham Lincoln was shot dead, the year Walt Whitman published his elegy "When Lilacs Last in the Dooryard Bloom'd."

The war was over, and the newly revived federal government, short on cash, passed a law requiring distilleries to pay taxes. While most in the business did their best to continue making whiskey under the table, so to speak, Jack Daniel was the first to register. The distillery is today the oldest registered liquor operation in the United States. He called his still Number One.

Today's twenty-one year olds relish the experience of walking into a bar and ordering up a shot of JD for the first time, legally at least. By the time Jack Daniel hit twenty-one, he'd been making liquor for twelve years.

On his birthday, he rolled into town and bought himself some new clothes: a black vest and frock coat, a clean white shirt, a black bow tie, some black pants, and a planter's hat rolled up at the brim. From that moment on, he wore the suit every day like a uniform (just as the original Jim Beam did), even when he had to put his hands to work in

Statue of Jack Daniel, at the distillery in Lynchburg, Tennessee. (© *2003 JunebugClark.com*)

the distillery. He was a little stump of a man whose hair thinned on top early, and he grew a massive goatee that, in the old pictures, makes him look like he tried to swallow a raccoon and didn't quite get the thing down.

Daniel liked women. And women liked Daniel. As one company spokesman put it, "He was considered the most eligible bachelor in Lynchburg. This was due to the fact that he was also one of the most wealthy men in Lynchburg, with a population of 361."

For a rural Tennessee man, Daniel possessed Joan Collins–like vanity. He was known to comb his hair incessantly. According to journalist Ben Green, author of *Jack Daniel's Legacy*, as Daniel aged, he dyed his hair, mustache, and goatee whenever he saw gray. He also lied about his age when he got older, which is why the date of birth on his gravestone (1850) is wrong. He never did marry or have any children. As his great-grandniece Lynne Tolley once put it, "[Jack's] love was always whiskey, done his way." (It would be the scoop of the century to be able to out him—JD BOSS LOVED LEATHER, POPPERS, AND COWBOY CULTURE!—but alas, there's no evidence.)

After the war, a lot of the local distilleries were ditching the time-consuming process that gives Tennessee whiskey its unique taste in favor of cheaper methods. They started making plain old American whiskey. But Daniel decided early on to run his still the old-fashioned way.

First the grain, mostly corn with some rye, was ground and cooked, then boiled in freshwater from the cave spring, forming what is called a mash. The distiller added barley malt, then yeast, which grew naturally on the barley, and the goo slowly fermented into a beer. Then he dumped the beer—9 percent alcohol at this point—into a still over a fire. The alcohol evaporated before the water, rising up in steam form through a series of copper tubes. (Distillation, folks!) The liquor that dripped out the other side was processed in the old-fashioned Tennessee way, the way Jack learned from the slave Nearest Green and the way that it's still made today, using the so-called "family secret." This secret makes for the difference between Tennessee whiskey and bourbon.

The clear liquor, drawn off at 140 proof from the still, is filtered through ten-foot cisterns filled to the rim with sugar maple charcoal. To make the charcoal, sugar maples are cut into two-by-twos, then stacked and burned to just the right stage. The cooled embers are finely ground. The liquor that passes through leaches out of the bottom drop by drop. It's a painfully slow process that takes as long as the entire distillation process up to that point. The sugar maple lends the whiskey just a touch of smoke and sweetness, and any impurities cling to the carbon in the charcoal. (Charcoal has this effect. That's why, if your dog ever drinks bleach or Drāno, the veterinarian will shoot charcoal down his throat with a great big turkey baster.) From there, the whiskey is aged in new oak barrels for at least four years. Finally, it's cut with water to the desired strength, bottled, and sold.

A portion of the leftover fermented grain mash—or sour mash—is added to the next day's fresh mash (back in the day, the rest of the leftover was fed to farm animals, the finest cattle feed in the world), to get the new batch fermenting faster. This sour-mash process, invented by Scot James Crow of Old Crow bourbon fame years earlier in Kentucky, is the reason why the Jack Daniel's label reads SOUR MASH WHISKEY.

Back in the early Jack Daniel's days, the whiskey was decanted into jugs and sold to locals throughout Moore County, men who cut it with water and sipped it slow—their own delicious little local delight. But as the years passed, the word on "Mr. Jack's" whiskey began to spread.

Toward the end of the nineteenth century, boozers in towns as far off as Nashville and Huntsville in northern Alabama began to ask for Jack Daniel's whiskey by name. Sales began to spill over into Georgia and Texas. Word might have traveled farther, but there wasn't enough whiskey to go around. In order to ensure quality, Jack Daniel refused to mash more than ninety-nine bushels of corn a day.

As the bottle began to replace the old jug in the Southern states, Daniel was on the lookout for something unique to set his whiskey apart from the others on saloon shelves. One day around 1895, a bottle salesman from Illinois showed up at Cave Spring Hollow with something that caught Daniel's eye. The salesman had tried to sell Daniel bottles before, but Daniel always turned him away. According to the legend, this time the salesman presented Mr. Jack with an oddly shaped square bottle.

"A square bottle for a square shooter," he said, flashing the salesman's smile.

Jack grabbed the bottle, looked it over, and nodded. It fit in his hand perfectly—a grip that made a man feel like he'd gotten ahold of something. It was a deal. Thus the unique square bottle you can swig out of today.

The early brand had no label—just a square bottle that held a quart of whiskey with OLD TIME DISTILLERY engraved in the glass and JACK DANIEL DISTILLER, LYNCHBURG, TENNESSEE engraved under that. In the middle was a circle with NO. 7 in it—the same number that strikes you when you see the bottle today. There are a half dozen theories as to what the number stands for, but nobody knows for sure. You might have heard any number of bullshit stories yourself—typical barroom fodder. Truth is, it's a mystery that died with the man. Perhaps seven was just his lucky number.

• • •

In 1904, Jack Daniel got his first break on the national scene. International, actually. That summer, the World's Fair—a gigantic festival displaying all manner of artistic and cultural exhibits from around the globe—was held in St. Louis. The organizers aimed to put the Midwestern city on the map. (Which indeed they did: the fair was later immortalized in the Judy Garland film *Meet Me in St. Louis*.)

In addition to the booths featuring eclectic foods and souvenirs, contests were arranged to award medals to creative people in the arts. One of them aimed to seek out the finest whiskey in the world. On the day of the event, international judges tasted from any number of the most esteemed whiskies in the world spread out across twenty-four long tables, including one Old No. 7, an obscure liquor from a tiny town three hundred miles to the southeast.

"Gentlemen," a bobble-headed judge slurred, once all the votes were tallied. A hush fell over the crowd. "The gold medal for the world's finest whiskey goes to Jack Daniel Distillery, Lynchburg—not Virginia, but Lynchburg, Tennessee!"

When the news reached Cave Spring Hollow, no doubt Mr. Jack— ever the narcissist—raised a toast to himself. He decided it might be a good idea to ship his whiskey to more competitions. The next year, Old No. 7 won a gold at a tasting in Liège, Belgium. There were more to come. In fact, Jack Daniel's whiskey has won seven gold medals in its time—three of them during Tennessee Prohibition.

Money was literally pouring out of the bottle. The spirit maker's spirits couldn't get any higher. But the luck was soon to run out. One day in 1905, in the office of the distillery, Daniel was trying to open his safe, a sturdy old three-foot-tall box on wheels with a combination spinner in the middle and Jack's name etched across the top as if the safe were a liquor bottle. He had a little trouble with the combination. The stubborn lock threw him into a bubbling rage; he reared back and kicked the safe good and hard with his left foot. It didn't crack, but Mr. Jack's foot did.

Days later, a gangrenous infection set in. You didn't really want a case of gangrene in the days before penicillin and aspirin. The infection caused the flesh to rot and putrify and it slowly crept into the victim's healthy tissues.

Eventually, a doctor amputated Jack's left foot. The operation likely involved a sharp saw, some assistants to hold down the old man,

FOUR JACKS—A WINNING HAND

What the JD distillery is offering today:

OLD NO. 7 BLACK LABEL: While the entire stable of JD whiskeys are made of the same ingredients—corn, rye, barley, yeast, and springwater (all of it distilled and charcoal mellowed)—the classic Black Label is aged four years in white oak barrels and bottled at 86 proof. Every classroom, office, and household in the land should be required to have a bottle of this uniquely American product.

OLD NO. 7 GREEN LABEL: This bottle's aged a year less than its classic older brother, and it's lighter on the liver (80 proof). It's also a couple bucks cheaper—if you can find it. The Green Label isn't advertised. You're more likely to find it in the South, especially around military bases.

GENTLEMAN JACK RARE TENNESSEE WHISKEY: Charcoal mellowed twice instead of once (a "double blessing," as tasters at the JD

and lots of Mr. Jack's old-time whiskey. (He liked it with a little sugar and a bit of crushed tansy leaf, by the way.) Nevertheless, the infection killed him in 1911. It was a slow and horrible way to die.

Because Mr. Jack didn't have any children, nephew Lem Motlow took over the operation. Motlow had been working at the distillery since 1887, so he knew the ropes. He was a hefty guy who wore circular wire-rim specs. He was also a tough guy who'd once shot a man dead on a Tennessee-bound train near St. Louis. Though he was astute, nothing could prepare him for what was about to occur in Tennessee around the time of his uncle Jack's death.

In 1909, the government of Tennessee outlawed the drinking and manufacture of liquor. In a snap, saloons closed their doors. Distillers and barkeeps set out looking for work as accountants, janitors, ballplayers, and hit men.

Lem moved the Old No. 7 still over the state line into Alabama, but Alabama soon followed Tennessee in outlawing liquor. He moved once again, this time to St. Louis, Missouri. There he launched a brand called Belle of Lincoln Straight Whiskey. A quart of liquor came in the trademark square bottle, with Jack Daniel's name on the bottom and the monogram JD in the center.

The Belle of Lincoln never took off, and the still went dry. Motlow

distillery used to say), this whiskey is smoother, a touch sweeter, and a little more approachable than the Black Label. As legend goes, Jack Daniel made this whiskey for his lady friends. First marketed in 1988, the liquor was the first new JD bottling in over a century. It's aged four years and served up at 80 proof.

JACK DANIEL'S SINGLE BARREL:

Most whiskies are bottled out of great big vats that hold any number of aged barrels full of liquor. This unique offering is the only single barrel Tennessee whiskey on the market. Like the name says, the stuff is pulled right out of the barrel (about 240 bottles to each one), cut with water to a fiery 94 proof, and bottled after six years. Different barrels might offer slight variances in taste (thus the barrel number printed on the label), though you'll need a bionic tongue to notice. The Single Barrel—the most expensive of the lot—tops out at $40 a bottle, well worth the price.

went into business selling mules and Tennessee walking horses and made a fortune. Eventually, he ran for state senate, and his platform was right on the money.

"Elect me and I'll do something for myself! But I'll also do something for you."

When the election rolled around, voters knew what was up Lem's sleeve. It took him four terms to deliver. Even though national Prohibition was repealed in 1933, Tennessee remained a dry state. But in the late thirties, Lem managed to pass a law that would allow him to start making whiskey in Moore County again. Selling the stuff would remain illegal—as it still is today. But he could make it and hawk it elsewhere.

In 1938, on the eve of World War II, Lem rebuilt the distillery in Cave Spring Hollow once again and started making Old No. 7 Jack Daniel's whiskey.

He began distilling roughly two hundred gallons of 86 proof whiskey a day—a small-time operation. The label was redesigned in favor of the familiar black label, with JACK DANIEL'S OLD NO. 7 in the forefront, and Lem Motlow's name listed as proprietor at the bottom. (It's still there.)

Lem, who by this time was balding and gray, had fallen ill in the late thirties, and eventually he was debilitated permanently. Navigating the rural distillery grounds was difficult in a wheelchair, so an African-

American man with big shoulders carried him around the joint, from the mash room to the cave to the office and back again. Lem micromanaged the entire process, tasting the brew at every step, all the while getting carried about by a heroic man who's since been forgotten. In 1947, Lem Motlow died of a cerebral hemorrhage—a terrible shame, considering the fact that Jack Daniel's whiskey was about to explode on the scene as the drink of choice for young starlets and old-time boozers alike.

In the fifties, well-known Americans began coming out of the teetotaler's closet, espousing their love for a little-known whiskey made in the hills of Tennessee—Jack Daniel's. At the time, Seagram's Crown Seven was far and away the most popular whiskey in the world. But this new brand's cult following was noteworthy to say the least.

With celebrities like Frank Sinatra blazing the trail, JD became the drink of choice for starry-eyed musicians. Among the big ones to follow: Jimmy Page, Etta James, Slash, Janis Joplin, Keith Richard, and Michael Anthony of Van Halen (who used to wield a guitar shaped like a JD bottle). The juice trickled into the general population's collective cup, intoxicating the masses for generations to come. The black label became synonymous with cool, style, quality, and badassness, to coin a word.

In 1956, Kentucky booze barons Brown-Forman, known for their signature Old Forester bourbon, bought the Jack Daniel's distillery lock, stock, and barrel. But nothing really changed at Cave Spring Hollow. Lem Motlow's sons were still pumping out whiskey the old-fashioned Tennessee way. By 1970, folks all over the world were sucking back one million cases of JD a year, compared to 150,000 cases in the early fifties. Today, American drinkers alone consume nearly four million cases of the stuff, making it the most popular whiskey in the country.

PART II

MARTINI MEN

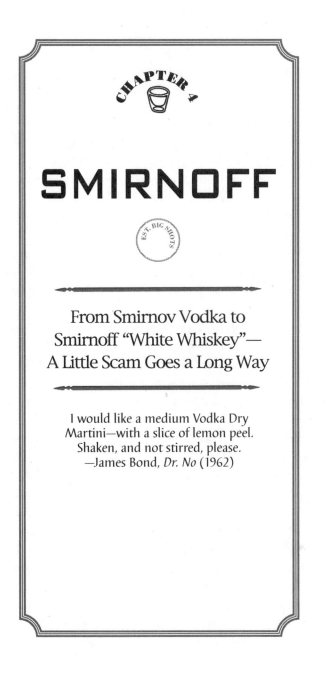

CHAPTER 4

SMIRNOFF

EST. BIG SHOTS

From Smirnov Vodka to
Smirnoff "White Whiskey"—
A Little Scam Goes a Long Way

I would like a medium Vodka Dry
Martini—with a slice of lemon peel.
Shaken, and not stirred, please.
—James Bond, *Dr. No* (1962)

et's cut to the, uh, chaser. Vodka is made for one purpose, and one purpose alone: to get you loaded. What else can you say about a "silent spirit" specifically distilled to have no flavor and aroma? The higher the quality, the less flavor! What else can you say about a liquor that can be produced anywhere in the world out of anything on hand—wheat, barley, rye, potatoes, beets, rice, molasses? There's even a new "snap frost" vodka out called Cîroc, made out of grapes.

Vodka is basically straight ethyl alcohol, which by law must be watered down. It requires no aging, so it can flow straight from the still to your swelling liver.

No wonder there are 2.2 million registered alcoholics in Russia—40 percent of the adult male population, 17 percent of the female—fifty-six thousand of whom are children under the age of fourteen. Roughly thirty thousand Russians die every year of alcohol poisoning. The average Russian drinks more than fifty liters of vodka per year. *Nostrovia!*

It's also no wonder that the vodka industry has played a huge role in the political turmoil in Russia over the past five centuries. From the moment Ivan the Terrible (who was in fact extremely terrible) took control of the vodka houses in the 1540s, leaders have recognized the enormous power distilled in the homegrown booze industry. Even today, as Nick Brownlee points out in his book *This Is Alcohol*, "one of Vladimir Putin's first actions when assuming the reins of power was to wrest control of vodka production from the independent manufacturers back to the state."

Countless casualties have suffered as a result of what might be called the vodka wars. Since Putin took office, for example, one of the nation's most powerful vodka merchants walked out of a shocking boardroom coup and had a heart attack. Putin's "economic crime police" have sent another into hiding and brought a third up on charges.

It's a common theme in Russia: the rise and fall of the vodka maven. And in the realm of these tragic figures, no one looms as large in the Russian psyche today as the two brothers who were arrested at their distillery in November 1917 when the Red Army stole the reins of the Russian government—Vladimir Smirnov and his brother, Nicolai. The

Smirnovs are two great symbols of what could have been in Russia, had the bourgeois managed to defeat Lenin's army in the revolution.

When the Bolsheviks installed Lenin in power, they turned the Smirnovs' distillery into a parking garage. Vladimir and Nicolai were imprisoned in a Ukraine gulag for being "enemies of the people." In other words, they were capitalists. Nicolai was executed. Vlad escaped and lived two more decades, only to die poor and unknown in France.

So how did the liquor that bears their name become what it is today—the ninth bestselling liquor brand in the world, the bestselling vodka in the U.S. by far?

The real Smirnov, the one responsible for the meteoric rise not just of the vodka brand but of vodka as a whole in America, wasn't named Smirnoff at all. Or Smirnov for that matter. He wasn't even Russian. He was a guy named John G. Martin, an English businessman who lived in Connecticut. The brand Smirnoff as we know it today hasn't been based in Russia since Lenin took over. The name aside, the major thing Smirnoff vodka has to do with the original Smirnov family is the "secret formula" for vodka production that Vladimir Smirnov supposedly passed along early in the twentieth century just before he died, a formula that might as well have been: make flavorless alcohol for the masses as fast as possible out of anything at all!

Smirnoff is a distinctly American product—one born out of an epic plot worthy of a Leon Uris novel, only funnier and not as believable. When John G. Martin died a very rich man in 1986, he must have taken great satisfaction in knowing that the entire vodka industry in the U.S. was born nearly overnight—to a large degree because of his own cockeyed marketing schemes. Although vodka was unheard of before WWII, Americans now drink more of it than any other spirit.

The success of the "flavorless whiskey" was the result of a grand comedy of errors that could only happen in America the beautiful. It was a series of bizarre coincidences that involved false advertising, anticommunist demonstrations, James Bond, the birth of the cocktail craze, and a steak sauce called A-One. It was all a ruse, and America swallowed it whole, along with a few Bloody Marys along the way.

The story of Smirnoff begins in 1815, when one Ivan Smirnov first founded the company I. A. Smirnov & Family in Russia. Ivan leased a cheap warehouse in Moscow in the remains of the old Wine Courts, devastated three years earlier by the French army in the Napoleonic Wars. He began distilling vodka and liqueurs. He registered the company in 1818 and found that Russians did indeed have an appetite for the hard stuff. By 1827, Smirnov had made enough income to build a new distillery near the Iron Bridge over the Moskva River—not far from the wreckage of the old Kremlin near the center of the city, where vodka is thought to have been invented five hundred years ago.

Ivan Smirnov started his vodka business at a fortuitous time. During the Napoleonic Wars in the early part of the century, Russian soldiers had marched all over Europe guzzling "water of life" as they pillaged. Populations throughout Eastern Europe formed a taste for it (the vodka, not the pillaging), and the demand for vodka spread. Smirnov's business took off like it was propelled by rocket fuel, which, in a way, it was. By the time he died in 1873, the family was already wealthy. Ivan's son, Pierre, rebuilt the distillery and opened offices at 2 Piatnitskaya Street, a landmark in Moscow that still stands today.

In 1886, Pierre set up a booth at a Moscow carnival to celebrate the brand's success. The Smirnovs' display featured live bears and bartenders dressed up in bear suits. In a moment that good capitalists spend their lives dreaming about, the gimmick caught the eye of Alexander III, the czar of Russia, and his entourage. As the legend goes, Alexander wandered into the exhibit, and a nervous hush fell over the crowd. He slugged a shot of vodka (*Nostrovia!*) and declared the Smirnovs the sole purveyors to the Imperial Russian Court.

On New Year's Eve at the end of the century, nobles and dignitaries were toasting Smirnov vodka with their pickled herring all over Russia. Some two thousand workers were churning out four million cases of the liquor per year at the distillery. The Smirnovs had fast become one of the richest families on the planet. But not for long.

Pierre died in 1901, and the company fell into the hands of his two sons, Nicolai and Vladimir Piotrovich Smirnov. The younger men had grown up rich and liked the finer things in life. They owned town houses in Moscow and country estates, bred racehorses, and drank vodka with aristocrats all over the world. In other words, they were prime targets when the communists seized Moscow in 1917. Lenin took control of the vodka distilleries as soon as he took power. He imprisoned the Smirnov brothers at Piatigorsk in the Ukraine and sentenced them to death.

Nicolai bit the bullet quickly. Vlad was luckier—the Bolsheviks decided to torture him before his execution. Five times he was marched from his cell to the firing squad, only to be escorted back. Then one day, Russia's White Army took the prison, and Vlad was set free. Leav-

A QUICK ASIDE ON THE DISCOVERY OF VODKA: Early manufacturers found one benefit to the extreme temperature in Poland and Russia: they could use it to make alcohol. During winter months, they distilled fermented liquid, made out of anything they had, by leaving it outside and letting it freeze. Because alcohol freezes at a lower temperature than water, the process would naturally separate the water from the alcohol. There you have it: vodka. Christian monks were the main producers. They masked the horrible taste of the crude liquor with dill, horseradish, lemon, birch (the precursors to today's flavored vodkas like Absolut Citron and Smirnoff Vanilla Twist). They used the stuff as medicine. It was also used as an ingredient in gunpowder, so it's ironic that they called the liquor shiznennia vodka, or "water of life."

ing all his possessions behind—millions of dollars, rare jewelry and art, a well-stocked liquor cabinet—he fled to Poland and eventually to France with just one possession: the recipe for Smirnov vodka.

After saving up some money, Vlad attempted to open a vodka distillery in France, distancing himself from his Russian heritage by changing the name "Smirnov" to "Smirnoff." Bad idea. The French made the finest wines in the world, not to mention cognac, armagnac, and absinthe. Trying to sell vodka to the French was like trying to sell sex to a prostitute.

On the brink of failure, Vlad Smirnov received a visitor from America in 1933. Rudolph Kunett was a Russian capitalist who, like Smirnov, had survived the revolution. Before 1917, Kunett's family had supplied the Smirnovs with grain for their distillery, so the two men were well acquainted. Kunett had since taken a job as a sales manager for the Helena Rubenstein Company in New York. Prohibition in the States had just ended, and Kunett saw dollar signs dancing across bars from New York to San Francisco and back.

Unlike whiskey, which had to age for years before it would be ready to drink (keep in mind the American whiskey distilleries had been padlocked for over a decade), vodka could be drunk right out of the still. Kunett made Vlad Smirnov an offer for his vodka's "secret formula," and Smirnov happily signed on. (It's worth noting that, in 1995, a Smirnov in Russia popped up and sued Smirnoff in the States, claiming that Vlad was a "rogue" and had no right to sell the secret formula. The judge heard the case while keeping a bottle on his bench, then promptly dismissed the claim.)

In September 1933, the Ste. Pierre Smirnoff Fils of New York incorporated. Kunett set up a small distillery in Bethel, Connecticut, and Smirnoff vodka was launched in the States six months later.

But Kunett ran into the same problem that Vlad Smirnov had in France. Americans drank whiskey and gin. There was no market for a grain spirit without much taste. Kunett tried to push the drink by noting that Smirnoff was once the sole provider of vodka to the Russian imperial court. But no one cared because the court no longer existed, and man, gin sure tastes delicious.

A close inspection of old cocktail books from the thirties reveals that a trickle of the Russian juice did dampen the barmaid's apron. A mention of the Vodka Cocktail (nothing more than a Vodka Martini) showed up in a 1934 issue of *Esquire*, and there were plenty of Eastern European joints in New York's lower east side in the thirties (as there are today) where you might've ordered, say, a Vodka Queen or a Russian Special. But no one was making a living off the stuff.

By 1939, as a *New York Times* article once put it, Kunett "was enjoying a notable lack of success." He was selling less than six thousand cases of vodka per year and losing his shirt in the process. He tried to sell the "secret formula" for $50,000, but no one would buy it.

Then one day in thirty-nine, on the eve of the Big One, Kunett met a Renaissance man who would come to be eulogized decades later as the man "who believed in products and ideas when few others did." His name was John Gilbert Martin.

The purchase of a vodka distillery in 1939 was an asinine business move by anyone's standards. But John G. Martin was a gambler and an iconoclast. An Englishman who'd been raised wealthy and educated at Cambridge before coming to America, Martin ran a Hartford-based company called G. E. Heublein and Brothers (the original Heublein was Martin's great-grandfather), a purveyor and importer of liquors and specialty foods. Prohibition had nearly flushed Heublein down the toilet. The company had managed to stay afloat by selling a product that had, by a fluke, taken off: A-One Steak Sauce.

In an era when businessmen wore top hats and dark baggy suits as a uniform, Martin wore an old hunting jacket. His colleagues described him as a man who went for risky investments for fun. Against all advice, he used profits from A-One Steak Sauce to acquire the Smirnoff distillery for a mere $14,000. He gave Rudolph Kunett a job, and a 5 percent royalty on every bottle sold for the first ten years. Right from the start, Martin hit a home run—with a corked bat.

One of Heublein's first clients was a distributor in South Carolina, who bought ten cases. A short time later, another order came in for *five hundred cases.* Martin decided to take a trip down south to see what was going on. That was when he learned that workers in his Bethel, Connecticut, factory were shipping bottles of vodka with corks marked "whiskey" on them.

"We had a salesman down there and he had put up a great streamer: 'Smirnoff White Whiskey—No Smell, No Taste,'" Martin later recalled. "It was strictly illegal, of course, but it was going great. People were mixing it with milk and orange juice and whatnot."

For a short time during World War II, right when the vodka train was just picking up steam, grain supplies were rationed and vodka production ceased. Martin served in the army in France and North Africa. He was eventually discharged as a lieutenant colonel, and when he returned to the States, he relaunched the vodka brand, trying to regain some of the prewar momentum.

In forty-six, he traveled to Hollywood to visit his fiancée, the actress Jane Weeks. While drinking in a bar called the Cock 'n' Bull, he had an idea. The Cock 'n' Bull was owned by an old friend of Rudolph Kunett's named Jack Morgan, who had been trying for years to sell a drink called ginger beer, which was popular in England. If the two men marketed their drinks together, they figured, maybe they could get somewhere. So, unaware that they were making history, they started mixing drinks, hunting for one with a signature flavor. After a few tries, they came up with a concoction they liked: a shot of Smirnoff vodka over ice with a dash of lime juice in a copper mug, filled to the rim with foaming ginger beer. They called the libation a Moscow Mule.

To market the drink, Martin bought one of the first Polaroid cameras and hit some of the best known bars in the nation. First he dazzled bartenders with the new technology; then he convinced them to let him take their photo while drinking a Moscow Mule. He always snapped two shots: one for himself and one for the barroom wall. Then he'd go to the joint across the street and lay a line on the bartender.

If everyone at Joe's Bar is drinking a Moscow Mule, then surely everyone here should be too, Martin would argue. Then he'd snap some more Polaroids and be on his way.

Slowly, sales started to take off across the country. As one re-

KNOCKOUT COMBINATIONS

One great selling point for vodka is its mixability. The so-called silent spirit doesn't overpower other ingredients, so you can mix it with just about anything: juices, sodas, bouillon, even cream and tomatoes for a pasta sauce. The one thing vodka probably shouldn't be mixed with is other alcohols. But for those who never learn, there are plenty of cocktails that call for vodka mixed with other liquors. Here are some of the most lethal drinks ever served.

RED DEATH: Two-thirds of a shot each of vodka, Southern Comfort, amaretto, plus one-third of a shot of gin and triple sec, and a dash of orange juice. Shake and then pour over ice in a highball glass with a twist of lime.

TROPICAL TEA: A half shot each of vodka, light rum, gin, triple sec, plus a full shot of pineapple juice, a third of a shot of cranberry, and a tablespoon of grenadine. Mix and serve in a highball glass over ice.

porter would later put it, "The Moscow Mule was a Trojan horse. It introduced vodka to the American people."

The Smirnoff brand hit a speed bump in the early fifties, due to the Red Scare. Joseph McCarthy's troops of paranoid pinko-phobic zombies took offense to the liquor's Russian heritage. The buzz led a crowd of New York City bartenders to gather and march down Fifth Avenue protesting Smirnoff. They carried a huge banner: DOWN WITH THE MOSCOW MULE—WE DON'T NEED SMIRNOFF VODKA. A photo of the mob with the banner landed on the cover of the New York Daily News the next day. Nervous Heublein employees turned to John Martin, wondering what their bossman would do.

"Do?" Martin later recalled. "It was great. All the people who saw the sign were rushing into the bars to buy the drink." In New York alone, Smirnoff sales tripled in one seven-week period in the spring of 1954. Clearly the fear of the Iron Curtain and the threat of nuclear annihilation wouldn't stand in the way of America's drinking.

During the fifties, the cocktail craze kicked off, and Martin rode the tide to riches all the way to the grave. The craze was fueled in part by the silver screen. As the drive-in penetrated small-town American markets, consumers got a glimpse of some of the drinks being served in Hollywood: fancy libations with exotic colors and classy accou-

GLASS TOWER: Two-thirds of a shot each of vodka, peach schnapps, light rum, triple sec, plus a third of a shot of sambuca and a dash of 7 Up. Mix and serve over ice in a highball glass.

SLOW COMFORTABLE SCREW: Two-thirds of a shot of vodka, plus half a shot each of Southern Comfort and sloe gin. Mix with a dash of orange juice and serve over ice in a rocks glass.

LONG ISLAND ICE TEA: A half shot each of vodka, gin, light rum, tequila, plus the juice of half a lemon and a dash of cola. Serve over ice in a pint glass.

THE ROYAL ALBERT: A shot of vodka, a shot of tequila, and a shot of Baileys poured into a pint glass half full of Budweiser. Serve with a ham-and-mayo sandwich on white bread.

trements, poured by the likes of Frank Sinatra and Humphrey Bogart. At the same time, the gender gap was folding, and women started accompanying their men to the bar, everyone ordering whatever cocktail was currently in vogue.

The bartenders making these drinks realized that vodka, since it didn't have the overpowering taste that whiskey and gin possessed, was much easier to mix. So they began churning out new vodka drinks, each place trying to outdo the one down the block. First came the Screwdriver (two ounces of vodka and 4.5 ounces of orange juice, garnished with a maraschino cherry if you're in the mood; the drink got its name from the engineer who supposedly invented it: he liked to stir it with a screwdriver). The Bullshot followed (one and a half ounces of vodka, three ounces of chilled beef bouillon, a dash of Worcestershire sauce, and some salt and pepper—all shaken with cracked ice and strained into an old-fashioned glass). Then the Black Russian (two ounces of vodka with an ounce of coffee liqueur and a couple drops of lemon juice served over ice). And finally the Bloody Mary (two ounces of vodka, five ounces of tomato juice, and a half teaspoon of lemon juice, served over ice with salt, pepper, and a stick of celery; add Tabasco and Worcestershire to taste).

By 1955, Heublein was selling more than a million cases of Smirnoff vodka a year. In the sixties, the company hit it big with a series of celebrity ads in glossy mags, with actors like Vincent Price, Buster Keaton, Zsa Zsa Gabor, Woody Allen, and Groucho Marx championing their favorite Smirnoff-spiked cocktail. Even James Bond, in *Dr. No*, got into the act when he ordered a Vodkatini with the famous line: "Shaken, not stirred." (Hitherto Martinis were poured almost exclusively with gin.)

John Martin died in 1986. By this time, "premium" vodkas like Absolut from Sweden, Finlandia from Finland, and Stolichnaya from Russia started giving Smirnoff its first real competition in the States. But the old faithful is still by far the bestseller in the world.

Today's production is a high-tech version of the old-fashioned one the Smirnovs employed back in Russia. Distilled in Michigan and California, the vodka's filtered through fourteen tons of charcoal to remove impurities. (Basically, it's flushed through a Britta water filter the size of a large house.) Six bottles of Smirnoff vodka are opened every single second, in more than 150 countries around the globe.

Not surprisingly, the story of Smirnoff vodka is served with a twist. When the Iron Curtain shattered in 1990 and the Soviet Union literally fell to pieces, the devastated ex-communist nation became a battle ground for hungry capitalists jockeying to gain position in the new market. Smirnoff vodka, the brand that had been banned by Lenin himself seventy-three years earlier, launched once again.

In May 1990, Heublein, who'd purchased the Smirnoff brand for just $14,000 six decades earlier, kicked off a $10 million TV and print advertising campaign with the theme "Back in the U.S.S.R." Just two years later, thirsty Russians were swallowing some five hundred thousand cases of Smirnoff per annum, for the equivalent of $5 a bottle. (Domestic brands were running a dollar apiece.) Status-conscious capitalists started shelling out barrels of rubles for silk Smirnoff ties, Smirnoff sunglasses, and Smirnoff baseball caps.

In Russia, "Smirnoff has really reached the point where it represents all that is chic and fashionable about America," one Smirnoff rep explained.

Talk about irony. You can only imagine how parched those two Smirnov brothers must be as they roll over and over in their graves for eternity—Nicolai and Vladimir, who died poor and penniless, their vodka brand stolen by Lenin only to be relaunched in America to astonishing success. If you've got a bottle in your freezer, grab it and pour a shot in their honor.

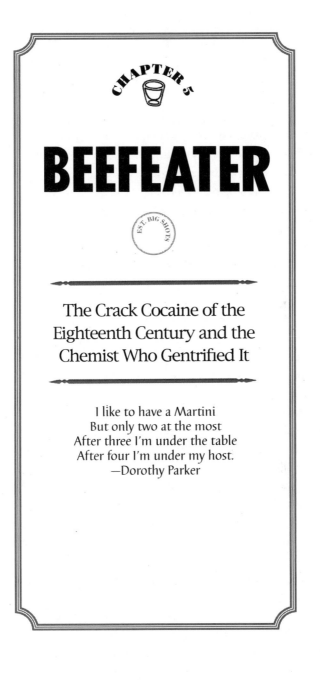

CHAPTER 5

BEEFEATER

EST. BIG SHOTS

The Crack Cocaine of the Eighteenth Century and the Chemist Who Gentrified It

---

I like to have a Martini
But only two at the most
After three I'm under the table
After four I'm under my host.
—Dorothy Parker

Gin was the first urban drug. It exploded on the scene among poor Londoners in the early 1700s. Nearly overnight, it transformed neighborhoods into ghettos, mothers into whores, children and fathers into sloths and murderers. The "gin craze," which lasted for thirty years during the first half of the eighteenth century, has remarkable similarities to the crack cocaine epidemic that swept through American cities in the eighties. By some accounts, it was worse.

Gin was first invented in Holland by the eminent professor and physician Franciscus de la Boe, otherwise known as Dr. Sylvius. He called it genever. When William III, a Dutchman, took over the English throne in 1689, he brought a taste for gin with him, making it the official "pouring spirit" in the palace at Hampton Court, where privileged folks began to call the banquet hall the "gin temple." Then William introduced the liquor to the masses. Big mistake.

Due to any number of circumstances, over the next two decades, gin made of dubious ingredients became the first liquor available in large quantities at cheap prices to the common man and woman. Up until this time, beer was the drink of choice among London's working classes. But by 1725, according to one government report, there were 6,187 "houses and shops wherein geneva or other strong waters [were] publicly sold." And this number didn't include the hags who sold gin in thoroughfares the way hot dog vendors sell their wares today—"in the streets and highways, some on bulks and stalls set up for that purpose, and others in wheelbarrows."

As Lord Hervey, a contemporary, described the gin craze: "Drunkenness of the common people was universal; the whole town of London swarmed with drunken people from morning till night." The city's population dropped drastically during this time. (There were some seven hundred thousand people living in London then, the equivalent of Columbus, Ohio, today.) Whole industries tanked as the working population, tanked as well, failed to show up.

Women actually drank more gin than men; that's why the liquor was known as Madam Gin or Mother Genever. Would-be mothers destroyed the fetuses in their wombs as they drank themselves senseless. (Who knew of fetal alcohol syndrome back then?) Even the hang-

Gin Lane, William Hogarth (1751). *(Image courtesy of the Guildhall Library, Corporation of London)*

men in town were known to be wasted while they worked on the gallows. At sunrise each morning, bodies lined the streets of bad neighborhoods—the living and dead. The gutters were filled with vomit and excrement.

The crude gin was brewed in common distilleries by hacks all over the city. In order to keep it cheap and still increase profit, as Samuel Johnson pointed out at the time, the distillers made their spirits "thrice the Degree of Strength required, by which Contrivance, though they pay only the Duty of one Pint, they sell their Liquors at the Price of three." Johnson warned that any attempt to deny the working class their gin would push them "almost to rebellion."

As neighborhoods began to collapse, journalists started reporting sensational accounts of gin-fueled urban blight. According to stories in publications like *The Gentleman's Magazine*, a predecessor to men's mags like *Maxim* and *Playboy*, boozers would drink so much gin that they would suddenly burst into flames, after which "their bowels came out." A dozen spontaneous combustions were reported in the eighteenth century in or near London. The apparent culprit: gin.

Alas, as historian Jessica Warner notes in her recent book *Craze: Gin and Debauchery in the Age of Reason*, gin, like the nasty neighborhoods where it first got a foothold in England, was destined to be gentrified. In order to quell the devastation in the streets and to ease the strain of the health crisis, British officials drew up the Gin Acts of 1729, '33, '36, '37, '38, '43, '47, and '51. Slowly, gin became tougher to come by. From 1700 to 1771, excises on the liquor grew 1,200 percent.

By the turn of the nineteenth century, only the well-off could afford the stuff. In response, a new group of distillers sprang up in London, men who aimed to make the finest-tasting liquor they could, liquor with integrity meant to be consumed by the educated class. The more refined the gin palate, the more refined the liquor itself had to be. The competition among distillers grew fierce, as several brands began to pop up throughout the city, fighting for their portion of the market.

Eventually, one of those brands was destined to win out, to become (in my mind at least) the finest gin ever made. It was known as Beefeater London Dry Gin.

If you pick up a bottle of Beefeater today, a formidable figure is striding as if he's about to walk right off the label. The man's dressed in an absurd outfit: a red, black, and gold cloak, red stockings, white gloves, bows at the knees and ankles. He's wearing a black hat and what looks like a giant powdered doughnut around his neck. (Keen gin drinkers will notice that the fellow on today's bottle—with a stylish goatee of brown hair—is considerably younger than the Santa Claus look-alike who used to be on the label. Looks like a focus group got ahold of this one.)

Also on the label, the name James Burrough is written—no fewer than ten times. So is James Burrough the guy in the ridiculous outfit? Did he like a chunk of beef with his liquor or was Beefeater the name of some happening nineteenth-century gay bar? Fact is, that guy on the bottle isn't James Burrough at all. In fact, the guy on the bottle has nothing to do with gin. He was dead long before the liquor gin was ever invented. More on that later.

James Burrough, the founder of Beefeater gin, was a young man from Devon who had a fascination with liquor and distillation. Burrough founded a small distillery on the river Thames in London way back in 1820. It was the very same year that, many miles to the north, one Johnnie Walker first opened a shop in Kilmarnock, Scotland, where he sold single-malt whiskies. What a banner year for alcohol.

Burrough and Walker had a lot in common, just as gin and whiskey do. Both liquors are indigenous to the place where they come from. In Scotland, whiskey emerged organically out of the ingredients available—springwater, grains, the peat used to smoke the grain. Similarly, gin is processed using a variety of exotic ingredients from all over Europe that, in James Burrough's day, would only be available in mass quantities in a major metropolis like London or Amsterdam. Of all the liquors out there, gin, like syphilis and Shakespeare's plays, owes the most to the modern city.

James Burrough was equipped to experiment in the strange sorcery of gin making. Like the early fathers of distillation, who saw liquor as a cure-all medicine, Burrough was a pharmacist. By the time he founded his distillery, he'd trained as a chemist's assistant in Exeter and worked as a pharmacist in Canada for six years. During his training, he'd already experimented with all kinds of strange alcoholic concoctions. He kept a diary containing recipes for bizarre drinks like English champagne and something called "artificial asses' milk." (The name alone makes the mouth water.) He'd created a pre-Prozac potion called "Sir Henry Halford's Recipe for Nervous People," which was probably heavy on the liquor, a substance that reduces inhibitions and tends to keep the hands from shaking.

But Burrough's real love was gin. His dream: to create the finest in London—a tough task, considering that the local competition at the time included guys like Charles Tanqueray and Alexander Gordon of Gordon's London Dry Gin fame. (The fact that you can go to a liquor store today and see these three sauces lined up next to each other on the shelf is simply awesome.) Burrough set up his operation right on the river Thames in the fashionable neighborhood of Chelsea, which was connected to downtown by King's Road.

At the time, gin wasn't the only game in town. Burrough distilled cordials too, such as blackberry brandy and rosemary liqueur. But gin was to be his bread and butter, and so he started experimenting. He kept a journal noting the different ratios of his concoctions. (That same dusty journal resides in the office of Beefeater's current master distiller, one Desmond Payne.) Gin takes its curious flavor mainly from

Beefeater creator, James Burrough. *(Image courtesy of Allied Domecq)*

juniper berries, which were once thought to have healing properties and were used to treat hemorrhoids and worms. But there are any number of other ingredients, depending on the particular brand. After several trials and errors, Burrough finally nailed his recipe, a process of gin making almost identical to the one Beefeater uses today. In other words, if you take a sip of the stuff, you'll be tasting a very similar liquor to the one that was dripping out of Burrough's still nearly two centuries ago. While the exact ratios of ingredients have always remained a closely guarded secret, the process has not.

First, Burrough made a neutral spirit, a liquor made of grain that comes out of the still "hot" and clear as water, similar to the way whiskey comes out of the still before it's aged in oak barrels, or vodka, or any grain alcohol for that matter. Then he dumped the liquid back into the still again. But before he lit the fire under it, the spirit was left to steep with other ingredients—mainly juniper berries from Italy, with dashes of citrus peels from Spain, almonds and coriander from Russia and Eastern Europe, and angelica root from the fields of Belgium. Twenty-four hours later, Burrough lit the fire again, heating the liquid so that the alcoholic vapor rose up out of the vat and into the copper tubing, drawing the botanicals' unique flavors with it as it trickled back out the other side.

Once satisfied with the flavor, Burrough turned to his next task. He had to come up with a name.

"A very large ration of beef is given to the warders of the Tower of London daily at court, and they might be called Beef-eaters."

So the famous quote goes. The year was 1669 and the grand duke of Tuscany was describing the hefty yeoman warders who had guarded the palace of William the Conqueror. William, the bastard son of the duke of Normandy, had conquered the Anglo-Saxons in 1066. During his twenty-one-year reign, William built the infamous Tower of London, just down the Thames from where James Burrough would later open his distillery. Outside the tower, the Conqueror stationed his guards. He dressed them up in a bizarre outfit, the very one that's depicted on the Beefeater gin bottle. These guards were paid in part with huge hunks of beef, to keep them portly and strong.

So there they stood, big guys whose job it was to hang out by a door and make sure the wrong kind of fellow didn't get inside. In other words, the guy on the Beefeater bottle is the forefather of that most fascinating and valuable of modern tradesmen: the barroom bouncer. They don't wear tights and velvet jackets these days. But goddamn it, they should.

To James Burrough, the name "beefeater" was a match. It symbolized the strength of his liquor—both in flavor and proof—and the history of London's greatness. In no time, sophisticated drinkers were muttering, "Beefeater," in restaurants all over the city.

For the rest of his life, James Burrough watched his gin business snowball. Late in the century, he handed the firm down to his two sons, Frederick and Ernest. By 1908, Beefeater outgrew the original Chelsea distillery, so they moved to a larger joint across the Thames in Lambeth. But the growth was just beginning. America was about to discover gin.

Up until this time, sloe gin had been available in the States; this strong-flavored liquor was brandy-based and flavored with sloe berries, the fruit of the blackthorn bush. The original Martini (the "Martinez Cocktail") called for sloe gin. But during World War I, U.S. servicemen got a taste of what our allies across the pond were drinking. After that, Beefeater's export market exploded. Bartenders in America soon started mixing Martinis with London dry gin, which didn't exactly hurt Beefeater sales.

Growth continued under the leadership of a third Burrough generation. Alan Burrough, who died in August 2002, was a one-legged phenomenon. (He'd had the other leg blown off in Africa during World War II.) He oversaw Beefeater as the liquor became the brand of choice for more and more gin drinkers. By the 1960s, it was the bestselling London dry gin in the world, accounting for more than half of England's gin exports. Today, it's number two, behind Gordon's.

These days, Beefeater is the only London dry gin that's still in fact compounded in London. The liquor's sold in 170 nations across the globe.

The success is partly due to good marketing. Who can ignore that idiot dressed up like a circus clown in tights, the prototype of the barroom bouncer, on the bottle? But Beefeater is also quite simply a fantastic gin. And there you have it: great liquor and imaginative marketing, mixed up in a glass. A perfect marriage.

MARTINI NATION

No cocktail in history has inspired such spirited debate and utter devotion as the Martini—that shimmering beauty of a libation, that glorious bowl full of diamonds. The oft-intoxicated sage of Baltimore, H. L. Mencken, called it "the only American invention as perfect as the sonnet." The author Bernard De Voto once declared the Martini "the supreme American gift to the world." (De Voto clearly forgot about the rubber chicken, which made its debut on a vaudeville stage in Newark, New Jersey, in 1911. But still, the Martini is a close second.)

Where did the Martini come from? Was there a bartender named Martini? A liquor purveyor? A notorious drunk?

Some scholars claim that the Martini was invented by an Italian bartender in New York named Martini di Arma di Taggia in 1912. Di

Taggia claimed to have served one of his signature cocktails to John D. Rockefeller. Not the case. As the noted liquor writer Barnaby Conrad III pointed out in a *Cigar Aficionado* article, Rockefeller was a teetotaler. And how would one explain the ubiquity of Martinis in Jack London's novel *Burning Daylight*, published two years before Di Taggia claimed to have invented the drink?

The Oxford English Dictionary claims that the Martini took its name from Martini & Rossi Vermouth back in 1894. This is also likely false.

The Martini's provenance is probably much closer to Jack London's hometown: San Francisco, the stomping ground of another famous bartender. "Professor" Jerry Thomas worked at the Occidental Hotel back in the 1860s. Apparently, he once mixed a drink for a gold miner who was on his way to the town of Martinez, a few miles east. Thomas recorded the "Martinez Cocktail" in his bartender's manual, published in 1887. Though the drink wasn't exactly a Martini, clearly it was a predecessor. It called for Old Tom gin, sweet red vermouth, dashes of bitters, gum syrup, and maraschino, chilled and garnished with a slice of lemon. The ratio was four to one. That's four parts *vermouth* to one part *gin*.

The transition of this drink to the Martini we think of today happened slowly over the years. Old Tom gin (which was much more juniper flavored) was replaced by London dry gin. The red vermouth was replaced with dry white vermouth. The bitters were eventually abandoned. Some bartender had the bizarre idea of tossing a couple olives in there, and later cocktail onions (for a Gibson). Slowly the proportions went to equal parts gin to vermouth. Then to two-thirds gin. "By the thirties, you find the Stork Club pouring 'em at an entirely reasonable five parts gin to one vermouth," notes the brilliant booze columnist David Wondrich, author of *Esquire Drinks*. "At the height of the Martini's powers, in the gray-flannel-suit years, the 'see-through' went something like eight parts gin to no parts vermouth, with an olive."

To this day, hard-core Martini fans can't agree on how to make one. And it's not just the proportions—it's the way the drink is mixed. Shaken or stirred? Whole ice, shaved ice, crushed, or cracked?

"You see, the important thing is the rhythm [of the shake]," noted the detective Nick Charles in the film *The Thin Man* (1934). "You always have rhythm in your shaking. With a Manhattan you shake to fox trot time. A Bronx to two-step time. A dry Martini you always shake to waltz time."

In the end, a Martini is whatever the hell you want it to be. Like a good set of tires, it'll perform beautifully whether it's dry (almost no vermouth), a little moist (a nice dash of the stuff), or soaked (equal parts). The only problem is communicating your exact preferences to a bartender. If you find one that makes a Martini to your liking, tip that barkeep nicely. When I was working at a particular fashion magazine years ago, my boss married a bartender. She fell in love with his pour, and the rest is history. (She was one tough broad. I imagine her bartender husband's out there right now, muttering the famous Bogart line from *Casablanca*: "Of all the gin joints in all the towns in all the world, she had to walk into mine.")

To wit, my Martini pour: three shots of gin with a half shot of vermouth, stirred with *crushed* ice and left to sit for a minute before it's strained. Then I pour the concoction into a thin-stemmed Martini glass, which has been chilling all day in the freezer, naturally. A couple olives later (the big kind, with a drop of the juice), and it's ready to drink.

CHAPTER 6

Martini & Rossi

EST. BIG SHOTS

The Shocking Truth
About
Vermouth

For a Cannibal Martini, take one-third
vermouth, two-thirds gin, and into this
drop a small girl named Olive.
—Fred Allen

You can only imagine the shock—the awe, the crushing blow to my epistemological foundation—when the waiter delivered my cocktail. It was years ago on a hot summer evening in Nice, that slice of paradise nestled on a sloping hill that leads down to the Mediterranean in the south of France. I was with two friends, sitting in a hole-in-the-wall joint we found in an alley filled mostly with Italian places. I'd ordered stewed rabbit and a Martini. While the chef busied himself hacking Bugs up and marinating his offal, the waiter brought my cocktail: a glass of sweet Martini & Rossi vermouth on ice.

"Whoa! Where's the gin?" I asked him. I could feel the tears welling up in my eyes. "THE GIN!"

"Che cazzo di Americano stupido," he muttered while walking off, most certainly to fill up my water glass out of the bidet.

But when I began sipping this cocktail, I was surprised to learn that it was delicious, a viscous mystery redolent of sweet wine but clearly different. It didn't have the boozy kick that I'd come to know and love from my Martini, that hurts-so-good right hook to the liver. But still, it was delightful, refreshing, and definitely intoxicating after a few glasses. This led me to ask my counterparts at the table, who were happily sipping Jameson: What the hell is vermouth anyway? Neither could answer.

Years later, when I started my research for this book, I began a quest to find a single American who could tell me what vermouth is. Though it is the second most important ingredient in the greatest cocktail on earth, I couldn't find a soul who could define it. And that is the shocking truth about vermouth: nobody knows what it is.

In Boston, where I used to live, I hit a place called Grill 23, a refined establishment on Berkeley Street that serves the very best Martini on the planet, bar none. (And believe me, I have done my research on this topic in cities all over the world—particularly in New York, where I currently reside.) Over the course of a few nights at Grill 23, I asked strangers cupping "see-throughs" if they could tell me what vermouth is. The results, out of fifteen subjects: nine "I don't knows," two "no ideas," one "wine gone bad," one "liqueur made out of pine," and one "wine made out of honey." Only one drinker came even close. A towering woman who needed a facial wax and a toothbrush (she'd clearly done her alcohol research as well) weighed in with: *"Wine mixed with some other stuff."* And there you have it.

Vermouth is wine infused with herbs, plants, the essence of fruits—the ingredients and ratios vary from brand to brand and whether it's sweet, dry, red, white, whatever. In this regard, it's like gin (and *not* like vodka), which is grain alcohol infused with similar botanicals. Thus the two complement each other perfectly. "Like a penis and a vagina," my favorite bartender used to say. Vermouth is usually bottled a little over 30 proof.

Hippocrates made the first vermouth some 2,400 years ago, or so goes the commonly held belief among liquor historians. The Greek physician created the drink as a panacea for the masses. That's about as good as medicine got back then. In the old days, a key ingredient was wormwood, the extract of which was known to kill off intestinal worms when ingested. The name vermouth comes from a bastardized pronunciation of the word wormwood. The Germans, who pronounce their *w*'s like *v*'s, pronounced it *vermut*—which you see ain't too far from *vermouth*. Wormwood was also used in absinthe until it was discovered to be addictive and highly toxic, thus its effect on worm colonies in the gut. It's no longer used in vermouth. Apparently, having intestinal worms is better than being dead.

The original vermouth was made with sweet wine that could stand up to the bitterness of the herbs. It was available in Europe for centuries, but like most alcoholic beverages consumed for enjoyment, it didn't really take off until recent times. The modern vermouth trade started in two places, and each is represented by one of today's most popular brands.

In the south of France, one Joseph Noilly began making vermouth in 1813. Noilly, along with other Frenchmen, believed that the quality of wine increased when it was transported in barrels on the bridge of ships at sea. The salty air and the sun gave the wine more body and a richer hue, the French claimed. Noilly created a vermouth and aged it in barrels in the open air near the Mediterranean. He created the first dry French vermouth, as opposed to sweet vermouth. His son, Louis, and son-in-law, Claudius Prat, later founded the company we know today, Noilly-Prat, thought by many to be the finest brand of vermouth in the world.

But the real vermouth frenzy occurred in a mountainous section of

VERMOUTH ET AL

What would the world be without vermouth? A world without a . . .

BRONX COCKTAIL: Two parts gin, one part dry vermouth, a dash of orange juice, shaken with ice and strained. Serve in a Martini glass and garnish with a thin slice of lime.

MANHATTAN: This drink was named after the Manhattan Club, which was a hot joint in (you guessed it) Manhattan in the early part of the twentieth century. Three parts bourbon, one part sweet vermouth, a dash of bitters, either shaken with ice and strained in a Martini glass or served over ice in a tall glass. Don't forget the cherry.

ROB ROY: Two parts Scotch, one part sweet vermouth, and a dash of bitters if you choose, shaken with ice and strained into a Martini glass, also served with a cherry.

northern Italy—in the city of Turin, at the heart of a region called Piedmont that borders Switzerland to the north and France to the west (and is known today for its delicious white wines and its great skiing). So many wine houses began producing vermouth in the early part of the nineteenth century that, in 1840, King Carlo Alberto decreed that producers in Turin and the surrounding hills had to register with the government.

Among these producers, one was to emerge as the world's best known vermouth: Martini & Rossi. The brand would be so successful, people would begin to refer to vermouth as Martini. It would become the Kleenex, the Cuisinart, the Xerox of vermouths.

In 1847, four ambitious men formed a company in Turin and registered it with King Carlo Alberto. Their names were Agnelli, Michel, Re, and Baudino. They called their operation *Distilleria National di Spirito e Vino* (National Distillery of Spirits and Wine), and they produced wine, vermouths, and liqueurs. Business took off right away, and they opened new branches in Genoa, Cagliari, and Narbonne during the following decade.

In 1860, Carlo Re died and Clemente Michel retired. The team was shuffled, and three new boss men emerged: Teofilo Sola, a bookkeeper; Luigi Rossi, an herbalist and vintner; and Alessandro Martini, a commercial agent. Martini had previously worked at a place called

HOLE-IN-ONE: Three parts Scotch whiskey, one part dry vermouth, a dash of lemon and bitters. Shake it all up with ice and strain into a cocktail glass.

RAQUET CLUB: Three parts gin, one part dry vermouth, four dashes of orange bitters, shaken with ice and strained into a Martini glass.

FOGGY MORNING: Had a tough night? Late for work? Time to whip up a healthy breakfast. This drink's got three shots of vodka, a dash of dry vermouth, bitters for the stomach (optional), peach juice to taste—all of it mixed and served over ice with a lemon wedge. *Bon appétit.*

the Bass Bar in Turin with a master bartender named Gaspare Campari, who would also go on to make a name for himself in the liquor trade. (For a taste of ruby-red Campari, see Part VI.) Martini understood the need for alcohol in daily life and the degree to which he could make money by selling it. Along with his partners, he continued expanding the company, which they were now calling Martini, Sola & Cia.

In Italy, most people drank the wines made in their region—the local *vino da tavola.* And in Turin, the vermouth competition was as stiff as the stuff itself. In order to market a brand, the three partners realized that they'd have to export their product.

In 1867, two years after the end of the Civil War in America, the first hundred cases of vermouth arrived in New York City. Taking advantage of a new infrastructure of railroads and trade routes, Martini, Sola & Cia also began shipping vermouth and sparkling wines throughout Europe, even Africa and Asia. These wines and vermouths began to earn an international reputation. Over the next ten years, the company would earn medals and honors for its vermouth at exhibitions in Dublin (1865), Paris (1867), Vienna (1873), and Philadelphia (1876).

Teofilo Sola died in 1879; the company renamed itself Martini e Rossi. By the end of the century, the company was Piedmont's largest exporter, shipping off more than three hundred thousand cases of vermouth a year. The company later fell into the hands of Luigi Rossi's four sons, and they continued growing the operation as demand for vermouth spread, especially in America, where the Martini as we know it today was invented. The company also began to diversify its liquor cabinet, buying up wineries in Europe.

By the 1990s, Martini & Rossi was dominating the vermouth market, hawking seventeen million cases a year. It was also the sixth largest producer of wine and spirits in the world, with any number of small brands in the portfolio, and some large ones too, such as Martini & Rossi Asti, still today the bestselling sparkling wine in America. (In 2001, Americans guzzled seven hundred thousand cases of Asti.)

In 1992, Bacardi bought out the company. That little vermouth operation that opened in Turin in 1863 went for $1.4 billion—and that was only for a controlling share, not the whole company.

Today at your liquor store, you can pick up four kinds of Martini & Rossi vermouth. The bittersweet Rosso (red) was the original vermouth, the only type available in the nineteenth century. Don't be fooled by the reddish-brown color—it's made with white wine. The color comes from a dash of sweetening caramel. This is the stuff you dump in your Manhattans. Extra Dry—the stuff that goes into a Martini along with the gin (or vodka, if you must, you charlatan)—launched internationally on New Year's Day in 1900 to much fanfare, a dry Italian vermouth to take on the French dry vermouths, particularly Noilly-Prat. Martin & Rossi Bianco (white) was introduced in the 1910s and is most distinguished by its distinct vanilla flavor. Rose, made with rose wine, hit stores during the Ronald Reagan years and carries deep notes of cinnamon and cloves.

What are the particular botanicals that go into each one? The company won't say. The mystery is part of the allure—think of it like ancient witch's brew, which in a sense it is. In fact, Noilly-Prat calls its blending room in Marseille the "room of secrets." While you may never learn those secrets, you can still experience the mystery in every bottle of vermouth.

PART III

SOUTH OF THE BORDER

CHAPTER 7

Captain Morgan

Pirate, Killer,
Drunk...
Rapist?

Ho! Henry Morgan sails today
To harry the Spanish Main,
With a pretty bill for the Dons to pay
Ere he comes back again.

Him cheat him friend of his last guinea,
Him kill both friar and priest—O dear!
Him cut de t'roat of piccaninny,
Bloody, bloody buccaneer.
—Unknown, Seventeenth Century

The first thing you should know about the real Captain Morgan: he never made rum. Although the labels on some of the bottles bear dates from the seventeenth century, when the real Morgan lived, Captain Morgan's Original Spiced Rum was actually launched by Seagram's in 1983. The brand name is a marketing ploy, and a good one.

The real Captain Morgan lived a century before a "brand" of liquor ever existed. He lived during a time when rum—a distillate made from the dross of manufactured sugarcane—was just becoming popular among sailors and explorers, and he drank copious amounts of it. In fact, Sir Henry Morgan liked rum so much, he drank it until his skin and the whites of his eyes turned yellow. He drank until his liver swelled up fat and hard like a bowling ball, so his belly was distended so far over his sapphire-buckled belt that he couldn't stand on his own two feet. The real Captain Morgan drank himself to death.

But before he did, Morgan lived a long life that makes for a tale as picaresque and hair-raising as any Hollywood script. If you judge by the picture of the smiley guy on the liquor bottle, you'd think he was a real swell guy, the kind of fellow who'd stop on the highway to help a stranger fix a flat tire. Hardly. The real Morgan was a privateer, a pirate captain licensed by the English monarchy to raid Spanish galleons and ports in the North Sea, as they called the Caribbean back then. Sailing from one sun-drenched island to the next, the swashbuckler slaughtered untold numbers of innocent and not-so-innocent people, torched entire cities, robbed from his own men, stole from priests and nuns, and changed the course of history forever.

By some accounts, he was a brutal rapist to boot. During his final years, Morgan got himself embroiled in a torrid sex scandal that's shocking even by today's standards. At the peak of his meteoric fame, the imbroglio sent him cascading off his pedestal into the quotidian hell of a London jail cell.

Nevertheless, by the time he died in 1688, Sir Henry Morgan had amassed an unfathomable fortune—huge caches of pilfered precious metals and jewels—not to mention a legendary status among centuries of salty dogs to come. All in all, he kept himself pretty busy, for a drunk.

• • •

Born in 1635 in the Welsh village of Llanrumney, Henry Morgan was raised near Cardiff, the capital of Wales. The stately family home where he was born still stands (it's since been converted into the Llanrumney Hall Hotel, with a pub on the first floor). At age twelve, Morgan set off on his first expedition at sea, bound for Barbados. There are two theories as to why. Some claim he was kidnapped and sold off in the white-slave trade, while others believe he was escaping imprisonment for brawling and—more urgently perhaps—the wrath of the father of a young girl he'd deflowered.

At the time, Spain had claimed most of the New World in the West for herself. One hundred fifty years earlier, the Spanish king Ferdinand had sent Christopher Columbus to what they both thought was India. Columbus had sailed the wrong way and landed in the Caribbean Islands, and the Spanish colonists followed. By the time Henry Morgan was born, Spain had brought in more gold from the West than existed in all of Europe three times over. And there was plenty more to go around.

There were laws in the New World—laws meant to protect the Spanish ports and the galleons carting the gold back to the monarchy. There just wasn't any way of enforcing them.

Spain's archenemy, Britain, launched a fleet of ships to infiltrate the rich island outposts. Headed up by Admiral Oliver Cromwell, the fleet was the precursor to the Royal Navy. In 1654, young Henry Morgan escaped from his slave owner and enlisted. He was dispatched to attack the Spanish at Santo Domingo on the island of Hispaniola (present-day Haiti). An experienced seaman, boozer, and brawler, Morgan impressed his peers in the pitch of battle. But the British lost this one, and the fleet retreated to Jamaica, where they set up their home base.

Morgan would end up making Jamaica his home for the rest of his life. It was there that he and his cronies realized that the straight-on military attack approach might not be the best way to go about things. So they devised a new plan. The era of modern piracy was about to be born.

In the years to follow, the British fleet began attacking and looting poorly protected Spanish outposts, rather than going after the military, as was the custom. It was piracy, a barbaric approach with total disregard for law or morality. Naturally, it worked. The pirates began hauling in so much loot that, instead of punishing them, King Charles II of England awarded them licenses.

The British already controlled some of the smaller islands in the

Caribbean, and they started to infiltrate more. (This accounts for the beer-battered fish and chips and bland meat pies you can order up today in Jamaica, Barbados, Bermuda, the British Virgin Islands, etc.) Meanwhile Morgan's reputation as a fearless raider earned him the title of captain, and he began a reign of terror that would mark his legend to this day.

Dressed in the classic costume of the buccaneer—an embroidered crimson coat and matching hat, with long locks of dark hair and a handlebar mustache that would make Freddie Mercury green with envy—Morgan looked much like the swarthy caricature on today's Captain Morgan rum bottle. According to portraits from the day, he had tanned leathery skin and dark executioner's eyes, which were a little too far apart. As captain, he chose his first target: the Spanish port of Cumana in what is now Venezuela. The town was renowned for its rich collection of fine pearls.

With a fleet of ten ships and more than a thousand men armed with sabers, muskets, daggers, and crude bombs, the British raiders took the Spanish settlers by surprise. They looted the city, taking whatever they desired, and escaped with massive amounts of gold. Next they hit Puerto Cubello 250 miles to the west. After that, Morgan sailed the fleet 125 miles farther west to the tiny town of Cora. As his ships approached, the settlers ran for the hills, leading Morgan straight to the mother lode, hidden there far from town. He made off with twenty-two chests of silver marked for the king of Spain, then worth £375,000—an unprecedented score, the equivalent of millions today. It was enough to make Morgan rich for many lifetimes. But he wasn't done yet.

Following the raid on Cora, Morgan made daring forays into what is now Cuba, Venezuela, and Haiti. One by one the ports fell: Providence, San Lorenzo, Venta La Cruz, Portobelo. At one point he sailed his fleet to a port in present-day Nicaragua, ventured up a river to a lake, and pillaged inland villages in the mountains. They were a fleet unlike any other at the time, driven by greed rather than patriotism.

In 1671, Morgan was promoted to admiral of all British warships in the Caribbean. He had a group of thirty-six vessels and more than two thousand men. He was known to torture local islanders until they gave up the hiding places of their gold. He held entire cities ransom and threatened to set them ablaze until the locals coughed up everything. He was recognized wherever he went—the most feared man in the Caribbean.

• • •

Captain Henry Morgan (1635–88). *(Image courtesy of the Mary Evans Picture Library, London)*

When he wasn't at sea, Morgan spent lavishly at taverns near his home in Jamaica, where he drank copious amounts of the local sauce—a clear crude rum that would likely repulse the palate of today's drinker.

Among other things, the Spanish colonists Morgan had been robbing had brought sugarcane to the Caribbean, which proved to have a perfect climate for the tall grass. Sugar was in great demand in Europe. A shortage of honey and the increased taste for sweetness among the upper classes (lemonade was invented in Paris in the 1630s) created an urgent demand for cheap crystallized sugar. By Morgan's time, cane plantations had popped up all over the islands, where they remain today. When the tall, thick cane grass was processed into crystallized sugar, molasses was left over. Clever sugar processors began experimenting with the molasses to see if they could make something useful out of it. When they added yeast and water, the molasses fermented. Eventually, some English subjects

RUM DECONSTRUCTED

Few liquors are as misunderstood as rum—the drink of pirates, navy men, and frat boys alike. There's good reason. For one, distilling regulations vary from island to island throughout the Caribbean. So unless you've done your homework, it's tough to know what you're drinking. The languages spoken among producers vary as well. You can buy Caribe rum with labels written in English, Spanish, and French. The liquor might be called rum, *rhum*, or even *ron*. This much is consistent: the liquor is distilled out of either pure sugarcane juice or molasses (what's left over after sugar is extracted from cane) and is generally bottled somewhere around 80 proof, unless it's "over proof" rum. The following will get you a grip on the bottle so you can pour accordingly.

WHITE RUM: The "see through" rum that resembles water—also sometimes called White, Clear, Crystal, Cristal, Silver, Blanc, and Blanco—is rum that's bottled young, aged either not at all or up to a year or two. White rum is usually the cheapest and not surprisingly the most popular of rum varieties. It's great for mixing. Example: Castillo Silver Puerto Rican Rum.

REGULAR RUM: Usually aged from one to three years, this rum will have an amber or copper color, a result of contact with the wood in a barrel. Caramel may also be added to enhance the color. Most regular rums (also sometimes called Gold or Oro) are good enough to drink on their own with a little ice, but they're also great for mixing—say, with tonic and a lime wedge. Example: Mount Gay Refined Eclipse Barbados Rum.

had the idea of distilling the fermentation the way whiskey was distilled back home. They called the liquor Kill Devil (because it was a cure for disease; it killed the devil in you) or Red-eye (it gave you a nasty hangover). Others called it rumbullion (from the English words "rumbustious" and "rumpus" because it made some drinkers violent—sometimes violently ill).

One published island diary that dates back to 1651, *Cavaliers and Roundheads Barbados* by N. D. Davis, had the following description: "The chief fudling they make in the island is Rumbullion, alias Kill-Divil, and this is made of sugarcanes distilled—a hot, hellish, and terrible liquor." Another contemporaneous diary describes rum as a dangerous beverage that could "overpower the senses with a single whiff."

A plague of drunkenness spread among seamen who were far

PREMIUM RUM: Generally speaking, this is a rum that's been aged for three years or more, also known as *rhum vieux* or *ron anejo*. Some premium rums are aged as long as fifteen years. Like a cognac or a fine single-malt Scotch, it can be sipped out of a snifter. Example: Ron Matusalem Gran Reserva.

OVER PROOF RUM: "Over proof" generally connotes any rum that's bottled at 51 percent alcohol or stronger (including the "151" that some producers market). It's usually white, and it'll jackhammer your liver if you're not mixing it. Example: Bacardi 151 ("Warning: Flammable").

DARK RUM: Also known as black rum, this stuff pours out of the bottle thick and tarlike. The color and viscous consistency is a result of the blending and aging process. Because it has a rich syrupy flavor, it's often mixed with other rums to give a cocktail (a Mai Tai, perhaps) an added touch of character and sweetness. Examples: Myer's Jamaican Rum and Gosling's Black Seal Rum.

SPICED AND FLAVORED RUMS: Like vodka, a rum's flavor can be infused with just about anything—orange, banana, coconut, pineapple, passion fruit, spices, coffee, even peanuts. Some folks dig it. But some think spiced and flavored rums are a bit silly—a mockery, a travesty, a sham even. My advice is to confront the issue case by case, bottle by bottle. Examples: Captain Morgan's Original Spiced Rum and Malibu.

from home, men who had pockets full of stolen gold, no family in sight, and plenty of time on their hands. Jamaica's Port Royal—once a lonely island outpost where Morgan and his men suffered through pestilence and ate dogs, rats, and snakes—became known as the "Port of Orgies," the most sinful and licentious city in the world. In the taverns, drunken sailors engaged in violent swordplay, sometimes wounding and killing each other in the name of amusement. Female African slaves who'd been imported to work the sugarcane plantations were made to dance, strip, and submit themselves on the tables and on the floor while others watched. Establishments were sometimes burned to the ground during a night's partying.

Among the island colonists, Captain Morgan was notorious for his ability to consume rum without showing any effect. Though by this time he'd married a Welshwoman, he enjoyed pleasures of the flesh like the others as well—though according to one biographer, he never fornicated in public. His ambition for drink grew to equal his ambition for piracy on the high seas. Eventually, his ambition would get the better of him.

In 1671, Panama City held the greatest cache of silver and gold in the world. Guarded with great resource, the precious metals had been smelted into coinage to get carted by galleons back to the king in Spain. The port was protected behind fortress walls. To attempt to steal the fortune would be suicidal.

Leading a massive gang of more than a thousand starving and hungover buccaneers (they'd had a terrible bout with some Peruvian wine they'd stolen two days before), Captain Morgan, then thirty-five years of age, landed on the isthmus of Panama in January and headed for the gated city of seven thousand Spanish settlers. The city's port was a silty river that dropped some twenty feet during low tide, and Morgan had already lost one ship—the *Satisfaction*—on a reef during the voyage. So the pirates landed at the village of Cruz de Juan Gallego and marched the rest of the way on foot, clearing thick jungle with machetes. Tribes of savages armed with bows and arrows greeted them. The Brits battled their way toward the city, scaring off the local warriors with explosive muskets, until they reached a hilltop that overlooked their destination.

There in the hills, they found livestock grazing. They hadn't eaten, they were brutally hungover, and they were about to go to battle. While some began slaughtering cows, horses, and donkeys, others busied themselves building fires to roast them. One pirate who was present later wrote:

They devoured [the livestock] with incredible haste and appetite. For such was their hunger, that they more resembled cannibals than Europeans at this banquet, the blood many times running down from their beards unto the middle of their bodies.

Below them, Panama City was laid out in a north-south/east-west grid. The city consisted of seven monasteries, numerous churches and convents, a hospital, and a courthouse. The streets were lined with homes made of sunbaked timber, which burned easily. The Spanish had received word of Morgan's arrival; a vanguard of 2,100 Spanish, African, and native soldiers with six hundred horses was preparing to fight off the British intruders. But it wasn't enough.

On a hot and sunny Sunday morning, Morgan attacked, and the clash turned into an inner-city riot. Citizens and military alike used anything they could get their hands on as weapons. The British sacked the city in a matter of hours. They slaughtered untold numbers, took three thousand prisoners, and then set the place ablaze.

By midnight, Panama City "was all consumed that might be called a city," Captain Morgan wrote in his diary. "Thus was consumed that famous and ancient City of Panama, which is the greatest mart for silver and gold in the whole world."

As the streets burned, the pirates turned their attention to their appetites, the kind men have when they've been at sea too long. One witness present—a buccaneer named John Esquemeling, who later published stories about Morgan's raids—described pirates raping scores of women in the streets in front of their terrorized families. The witness recounted one specific incident regarding Morgan himself.

The captain allegedly captured the wife of a rich merchant, a beautiful and virtuous woman. He cornered her, and according to Esquemeling, who claimed to have been within earshot of the incident, she begged him to kill her rather than rape her.

"Sir," she pleaded, "my life is in your hands; but, as to my body in relation to that which you persuade me unto, my soul shall sooner be separated from it, through the violence of your arms. . . ."

According to the witness, Morgan then ravaged her: "He used all the means he could both of rigour and mildness to bend her to his lascivious will and pleasure."

Morgan looted Panama City for a total of twenty days, then absconded with literally boatloads of loot. Little did he know, the kings of Spain and Britain had just signed a peace agreement back in Europe. Even had they not, Morgan's murderous assault was excessive. Just forty-four days after the raid, a broadside hit the streets of London detailing the shocking fall of Panama City. News of the sexual exploits followed, courtesy of John Esquemeling. If Morgan went unpunished, the Spanish were prepared to form an army of five thousand men to sail on thirty-six ships, intending to capture Jamaica from the English at all costs.

Charles II immediately declared martial law in Jamaica, and within weeks, Captain Morgan was arrested and brought back across the At-

Morgan Sacks the Town of El Puerto Del Principe. (Image courtesy of the Mary Evans Picture Library, London)

lantic in chains. A long investigation ensued, during which time Morgan was the subject of public consternation and ridicule. He was humiliated—Bill Clinton–style.

Luckily for Morgan, Charles II was himself an accomplished sailor and carouser. It appears that Morgan and the king boozed it up good and hard together during the captain's prison term. Morgan, in turn, sued Esquemeling for accusing him in print of rape and other crimes. He ended up winning the case, the first ever libel court case of its kind.

After two years, the buccaneer was exonerated, sent back to Jamaica, and awarded lieutenant governorship of the island. He was later knighted. His legend made, the cloud of controversy burned away under the hot Caribbean sun, and he had nothing left to do but drink himself to death.

For the next fifteen years, Morgan spent his days heading from tavern to tavern, boasting of his exploits and making new enemies. The drunker he got, the more bizarre were his antics. On May 14, 1682, he was removed from his post as lieutenant governor for his consistent "irregularities."

As the pirate moved into his fifties, his health started to decline. In April of Morgan's final year, one Dr. Sloane came to see him and wrote in his notes that the captain looked "lean, sallow-coloured, his eyes a little yellowish and belly jutting out. He had a kicking or roaching to vomit every morning." The culprit, Sloane gathered: "drinking and staying up late."

The doctor urged temperance, and Morgan improved when he stopped drinking. But he couldn't control himself for long. In his final months, his legs started to swell (a symptom of the liver disorder gout), and his gut followed. Eventually, his liver ballooned. He was in such pain he could barely move from the hammock on the veranda of his mansion in Jamaica's Port Maria.

At eleven in the morning on August 25, 1688, the buccaneer died at the age of fifty-three. His bowels were removed and buried beneath the altar of the church in Spanish Town. (It must've seemed like a good idea at the time.) The rest of his body was sent back to Wales for burial.

A shady dealer, Morgan left behind more than a reputation as a drunken pirate king. On a number of his brutal raids, he made off with large amounts of booty and afterward refused to pay his men their full share of the loot. Or so his buccaneers suspected. Whether this is true or not, the man brought in an enormous fortune during his lifetime. In the lawless islands, banks were dubious, and they didn't issue checks or ATM cards. If you had in your possession enough stolen goods to fill up the Coliseum in Rome, you had to figure out a place to stash it. So what happened to Morgan's loot?

There's evidence to believe that he hid a large quantity of gold and silver in caves near his plantation in Jamaica and in Cayo Zapatillas in Panama, as well as back in Wales near where he was born. Any number of expeditions have been launched over the centuries to gather the loot. None of it has ever been found.

THE SKINNY ON CAPTAIN MORGAN'S RUM

- The Captain Morgan Rum Company was founded in 1943, and was later purchased by Seagram's.

- Captain Morgan is second in rum sales in the world, behind Bacardi.

- Drinkers consume about thirty-five million bottles of Captain Morgan's rum annually.

- The brand is now owned by Diageo, the liquor behemoth that also owns Smirnoff, Guinness, Baileys, Johnnie Walker, and a host of other tasty beverages.

- The rum is produced at the Distileria Serralles in Puerto Rico, though the Captain Morgan rum that's drunk outside the U.S. is produced in Jamaica.

- There are five Captain Morgan spiced rums currently on shelves, aimed at different rum categories: Silver Spiced (white rum), Original Spiced (regular rum), Black Label (dark rum), Private Stock (premium rum), Parrot Bay Coconut (flavored rum).

However, in 1999, a crew from an underwater documentary company out of Halifax, Canada, was filming on a shipwreck off the coast of Haiti when they came across the ruins of another boat under just six feet of seawater. After investigating the wreck and checking archaic records back in Britain, the crew learned that the ship was in fact the *Merchant Jamaica*. It was Sir Henry Morgan's boat—the only seventeenth-century pirate ship ever to be found.

According to records, the *Merchant Jamaica* struck a reef while sailing along Haiti's southwestern coast in the 1670s. The ship broke apart in the shallows. Eighteen men perished, but Morgan survived and kept notes on what happened. He later returned to retrieve twenty cannons (nine remain with the wreck).

"We have already found the anchor and the cannons and a few pieces of porcelain and some bronze coins," Monika Wetzke, a spokesperson for the expedition, told a newspaper in Morgan's native Wales. "We haven't found any bodies."

Or any loot either. Whatever Morgan had up his sleeve, it's still out there—a modern-day pirate's treasure so huge it could only be equaled by, say, a brilliantly marketed brand of liquor that sells some thirty-five million bottles a year. As they say at sea, down the hatch.

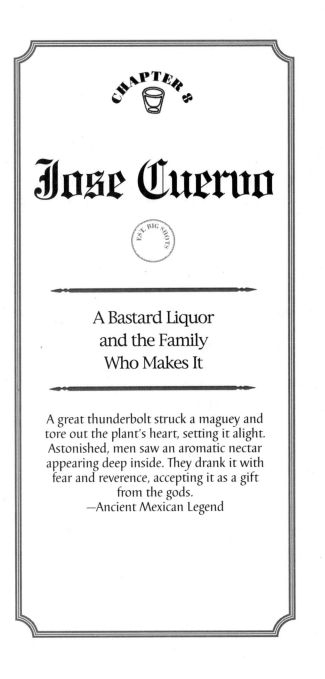

CHAPTER 8

Jose Cuervo

EST. BIG SHOTS

A Bastard Liquor
and the Family
Who Makes It

A great thunderbolt struck a maguey and
tore out the plant's heart, setting it alight.
Astonished, men saw an aromatic nectar
appearing deep inside. They drank it with
fear and reverence, accepting it as a gift
from the gods.
—Ancient Mexican Legend

Closing time. All the dancing girls are gone. The shot glasses are empty. The disco lights have faded, leaving only the nauseating glare of neon and the stink of cleaning fluid coming off the mop that a coked-up janitor is banging up against my toes under the table.

We're sitting in front of an empty stage at a Guadalajara strip club in the heart of tequila country in Mexico, just seconds before sunrise. A drunken crowd is filtering out. "Everything is slowly dribbling back to the sewer," as one writer once said about the dawn. "The day is sneaking in like a leper. . . ." To my left, a journalist named Scott is slurring something about a flight to New York we're meant to catch in an hour. On my right, a guy named Reyno is sitting with his jaw ajar. His head looks like a cash register with the door open. *Ka-ching!* All the money's gone.

Reyno grunts and points at a woman who is walking down an aisle toward us. Clearly she's not one of the lovely dancing girls we've been enjoying. When she gets to the table, it's evident that she is at least eight months pregnant.

"Hmm," she says. "You speaka da Inglais, *riiighhttt?*"

She sticks her cigarette in her mouth and puckers her lips. The ember burns a bright gold. When she flashes a hockey player's grin, the smoke streams from the gap where one would assume a front tooth used to be. She's wearing a stained white T-shirt, a baggy purple skirt, and running shoes; her straight jet black hair is pulled back into a ponytail. Her pregnant breasts are swollen and saggy.

"Yes," Reyno answers. "We speak English."

"You have hotel?"

"Well," he answers, "we don't, like, own one. But we have rooms, right down the road."

"Two hundred dollars," the pregnant woman says calmly, as if she were a tollbooth operator asking for a highway fee. "All three of you. *Righhttt?*"

Now what happened next is off the record. (Suffice to say we didn't have the $200, which was fine by all accounts.) The story is meant to illustrate the kind of situation a person can find himself in after drinking tequila for ten hours straight. This is, after all, a chapter about Jose Cuervo—the man, the mystery, the liquor. Rest assured, there's more to the Cuervo story than dancing girls and toothless whores.

We began the day early in the morning, drinking chilled glasses of lemonade while strolling through the rugged blue agave fields of a town called Tequila in the state of Jalisco, Mexico. We were following in the footsteps of one Jose Antonio de Cuervo, who walked the same fields over two centuries earlier. Later, we toured the Cuervo distillery, La Rojena, where we marveled over the decadent collection of antique leather saddles and theater masks and watched the process by which tequila is made. We also tasted some of the family's remarkable private reserve, their attempt to make the finest sipping tequila ever made, down in their liquor cellar—a creepy stone cave that's reminiscent of the death chamber in Edgar Allan Poe's "Cask of Amontillado."

By day's end, we'd taken in the whole story of Jose Cuervo, from the beginning all the way to the end. As far as stories go, the Cuervo tale's a good one—a uniquely Mexican story, about the rich as well as the destitute, about the Spanish conquistadors, about love, war, parasites, and all manner of things under the hot sun. But most of all, it's a story about making great liquor. And then drinking it.

The Jose Cuervo story begins way back in the days before Cortez and the Spanish conquistadors pillaged the New World. Millennia ago in the harsh highlands of what is now Central Mexico, natives discovered a juice that oozes from the heart of a wild lily that grows in the dry soil amid evergreens and juniper trees. The Aztecs called the wild plant maguey. With sharp shoots of crisp blue-green leaves darting into the sky, the maguey resembles the green top of a pineapple, or some wild punk rock hairdo from the Sex Pistol days. Only the lily can grow eight feet high, as if its sharply pointed edges are the earth's weapons, battling a relentless sun.

When the heart of the maguey is cooked and pressed, it bleeds a rich crystalline liquid, slightly sweet and acidic. If it's not drunk right away, natural yeasts help to ferment the sugars, turning the liquid into a beverage a little stronger than beer. Natives called the drink *pulque*. For the Aztecs, the maguey was a representation of Mayahuel, a goddess who had four hundred breasts, which dripped an intoxicating milk. Much toil went into the creation of a brassiere for this mythical character, but that's another story.

Tequila v. Mezcal

No, they're not the same thing. Yes, they both get you fired up.
So what's the difference?

TEQUILA   V.   MEZCAL

RULES AND REGULATIONS

The tequila industry is regulated by the Mexican government, just like wine is in France. The liquor must be made from 100 percent natural ingredients, with at least 51 percent reduced sugars from the Blue Agave plant. High-quality tequila will say 100 PERCENT BLUE AGAVE on the label.

Mezcal is not regulated, so you never know what's really in it. It's generally made from other agave varieties such as Espadin, Mano Larga, and Bermejo. This is not to say that there's no such thing as high-quality mezcal.

HOME FIELD ADVANTAGE?

By law, tequila must be made from agave grown in certain regions of Mexico: Jalisco (where the town Tequila is), Guanajuanto, Michoacan, Nayarit, or Tamaulipas. It must be bottled in Mexico.

Mezcal can be distilled and bottled anywhere. Most of it comes from Oaxaca.

STEAMED, ROASTED, OR SMASHED

To make tequila, distillers steam the "pina" (the trimmed heart of the agave plant) inside adobe ovens to convert the starches into sugar for fermentation.

To make mezcal, distillers *roast* the pina.

After the Spanish conquered the Aztecs in the 1520s, the Spanish captain Cristobal de Onate founded the town of Tequila (even though it had been there for centuries) on April 12, 1530. Historians argue about the etymology of the word "tequila," but it appears to come from the native *tequitl,* meaning work or job.

Onate owned vineyards back in Spain, and he had a taste for alcohol. In no time, he and his cohorts discovered the tangy buzz of *pulque.* They called it *aguamiel* (honey water). Back in Europe, the Spaniards had been distilling wine into brandy for ages. When they

TEQUILA   V.   MEZCAL

ONCE BITTEN, TWICE DISTILLED

Tequila is distilled twice; so the product is usually pretty pure, especially if it's 100 percent Blue Agave.

Mezcal is distilled once.

WORMS

There's no worm in tequila.

Mezcal sometimes has a worm in it—the gusano, which is a parasite that lives in agave plants. Why? Some say it's to ward off evil spirits. For the most part, it's a marketing gimmick aimed at people dumb and/or drunk enough to swallow a friggin' worm.

THE FINE PRINT

Tequila bottles tell you how the liquor's been made. If it says 100 percent Blue Agave, you're much less likely to wake up in the morning in a Mexican prison with a tattoo that says JUAN PHILLIPE on it.

Mezcal bottles don't usually give you much info. Unless you're buying a reliable brand that you know well, you have no idea what's in a bottle. Proceed with caution. But don't be fooled. There is some fantastic mezcal out there. Try Del Maguey or Beneva.

brought copper stills over from Spain and distilled *pulque*, the liquor tequila resulted, a bastard booze born out of the strife between the Spanish conquerors and the native Mexican Indians.

In the 1620s, one Spanish settler named Domingo Lazaro de Arregui wrote of the maguey and its dangerous powers, in what is considered the first historical reference to tequila:

From these same leaves, [the natives] are able to squeeze out a juice from which, little by little, they obtain wine, clearer than water, stronger than moonshine, and of the same taste. And although the mezcal from which it is produced confers many virtues, the vulgar and excessive manner in which it is consumed, debases the wine and even the plant.

Now, not to harp on this Mayahuel myth, but if you took a woman with four hundred breasts with nipples that oozed liquor and stuck her on a bar, is it any wonder that things were getting out of control?

The Spanish settlers quickly realized that the maguey liquor was a coveted resource that could be sold and bartered and perhaps used to keep the natives loaded and quiet. So they sent experts over from Europe to study the plant. One Swedish botanist at the time catalogued the maguey as *agave* or *agavaceas* (referring to the Latin word *agavus*, which means "illustrious"). The name stuck; the plant is still called agave today.

In 1758, the king of Spain granted a parcel of land to a man so that he could begin cultivating agave. This man would become the world's first mass producer of tequila. His name was Jose Antonio de Cuervo.

From this point on, the history of the name Jose Cuervo entwines itself with the history of Mexico as a nation. There is no single man to whom the tequila's name is indebted. There are a number of Jose Cuervos, generations of men who shared a name and a passion for distilling some of the finest tequila in Mexico for centuries.

The original tequila producer, Jose Antonio de Cuervo, saw his operation shut down in 1785, when King Charles III outlawed liquor in Mexico, likely after seeing what this fierce juice could do to people who weren't prepared for its debilitating effects. Wander into any frat house at any college in America on a Friday night, and you can at least understand where he was coming from. But a decade later, a new Spanish king, Carlos IV, took over and lifted the prohibition. He granted the second Jose Cuervo, Jose Maria Guadalupe Cuervo, the first license to produce tequila commercially. This second Cuervo rebuilt his father's distillery—the *Confradia de las Animas hacienda*—and started producing tequila again.

In the early 1800s, the Mexicans took on the Spanish in a bloody battle for independence. Before heading into the fray, it seems, the rebels got themselves good and wasted. A drunk man can hold a gun a lot more steadily than a nervous man can. Then they went nuts, shot at anything that moved, and died in droves. Liquor played a huge role in Mexico's war for independence, and not just on the battlefield. It was used as liquid courage and to treat the wounded, and it was seen as a panacea for the masses. According to the *Diario de Mexico*, published in 1812, tequila was known to cure illness, to aid during childbirth, and to ease the pain of menstruation, "even increasing its flow as desired." The liquor "kills worms and prevents other parasites from spreading," the book said, which is a good thing if you think about it. (These worms are not the same species found in bottles of Mezcal today, which is also a good thing.)

As tequila's popularity spread, Jose Maria Guadalupe Cuervo's distillery grew exponentially. He owned a family house, a production facility, and twelve fields with thousands of agave plants. The dusty town of Tequila was quickly becoming one of the richest in the area. When Cuervo died (he wouldn't be the last Jose Cuervo to light a fire beneath a still), the operation fell into the hands of his daughter's husband, Vincente Albino Rojas, who renamed the distillery La Rojena, which it's still called today.

For the rest of the nineteenth century, La Rojena continued to expand, despite political instability. Tequila became a staple resource, part of the local economy and diet. In the fields, workers on horseback tied gourds full of the liquor to their saddles. For shot glasses, they used carved-out bull horns, which they tied around their necks with a string of leather. They were adept at pouring the liquor into the horn and swigging without spilling, all with one hand, while keeping the other on the horse's reins and riding through the fields. That's like drinking a shot with salt and lime all with one hand without spilling—while driving a stick shift in heavy traffic. Not recommended.

Money and booze were plentiful. Things were rolling along splendidly.

Late in the century, a man named Jose Flores took over La Rojena. Up until that time, tequila was stored in wooden casks and ladled into smaller casks for transport. Flores was the first to bottle it. In 1880, he was selling two thousand liters of tequila every day. He took advantage of the new railroad and began exporting the stuff, sending a third of his total production over the border to the United States and some more to South America and the United Kingdom.

At the turn of the twentieth century, Jose Flores died. He left everything to his wife, Ana Gonzalez Rubio, who was young enough to marry again. In 1900, she found a new husband. His name? Jose Cuervo.

ROLL OUT THE BARREL!

Heading to the liquor store? Here's a breakdown on the four different kinds of tequila, with Cuervo's contributions included.

🥃 **WHITE OR SILVER (BLANCO OR PLATA):** This colorless tequila's pretty much what comes out of the still. It's aged a maximum of thirty days in an oak barrel, sells for pretty cheap, and tastes like firewater. Cuervo doesn't make a bottle of white tequila, which is fine. You're better off spending the extra couple bucks anyway on some . . .

🥃 **GOLD (JOVEN):** This liquor's a blend of tequilas, similar to a blended Scotch like Johnnie Walker in that regard. It's usually Reposados (see below) "married" to a small amount of White Tequila. Example: Jose Cuervo Especial (or "Cuervo Gold" as it's known), the most popular tequila in the world.

• • •

The latest incarnation of the liquor's namesake—Jose Cuervo Labastida, a direct descendant of the Cuervo who started the operation back in 1758—was the first to brand the drink under his own name. He trademarked his operation JOSE CUERVO'S GREAT MEZCAL FACTORY IN TEQUILA. The liquor was simply called Cuervo.

At the time, there were eighty-seven distilleries in the region of Jalisco, most near the town of Tequila. But Cuervo was the largest. (The second largest was Sauza; the two competitors are still numbers one and two today. Back then, the families feuded about politics as well as their share of liquor sales.) This new Jose Cuervo had a lot of cash by anyone's standards. At the turn of the twentieth century, he owned fields with four million agave plants, plus 280 mules and horses and 112 pairs of oxen. He owned a mansion in the city of Guadalajara. The trip to Tequila from Guadalajara took twelve hours by coach over treacherous territory; the unpaved and dusty roads wound through long stretches of agave fields. To invigorate the horses pulling the cart, drivers would fill their mouths with tequila and blow it up the animals' noses.

"Upon arrival in Tequila, the whole town hall would be present to welcome my aunt and uncle," Jose Cuervo Labastida's nephew would later write. Not only did Cuervo employ a significant portion of town, he brought piped water to Tequila. If you've ever awoken after a night

🥃 **RESTED (REPOSADO):** This stuff gains a golden hue, as it ages in charred oak casks for two to twelve months. Generally speaking, Reposados are mellower in flavor than White Tequilas. Example: Jose Cuervo Tradicional, the oldest member of the Cuervo stable. This authentic 100 percent agave liquor's very similar to what Jose Antonio de Cuervo was making back in the 1760s.

🥃 **AGED (ANEJO):** The cognac of tequilas, Anejo is meant to be sipped rather than shot. Aged over a year at the minimum in oak barrels, it features a dark amber color and a rich full flavor that'll linger on your tongue and in your throat. Example: Cuervo's Reserva de la Familia, a blend of Anejos that average five years of age. Thirsty? You'd better whip out the plastic; this bottle will run you a hundred beans or more.

of drinking Mexico's finest export, you can only imagine the thrill of having some running water in your home for the first time to cool your head.

In town, however, the Mexican way of life began to show some strain. As one Cuervo descendant noted about the village of Tequila at this time, "No self-respecting gentleman was considered dressed without a pistol in a nail-studded holster and a wide belt to carry the munitions. Scores were settled late at night, after observing the peaceful hour of the serenade."

On November 20, 1910, a populist named Francisco Madero led an insurrection to overthrow Mexico's dictator General Diaz. The fabled Mexican Revolution had begun. The war was essentially the poor against the rich, the have-nots against the haves, with provincial guerrilla leaders like Pancho Villa in the north and Emiliano Zapata in the south leading the disorganized masses.

Once again, Cuervo's tequila fueled the rebels on Mexico's battlefields. Tequila became known as "the drink of the trenches." Revolutionaries guzzled the stuff as they stormed town after town, battling with six-shooters, dying drunk in the dust.

When the rebels raided the city of Guadalajara, they made the long trip to La Rojena in Tequila and "confiscated" barrels upon barrels of Jose Cuervo Labastida's liquor. They mixed the hard stuff with fruit juice and drank themselves into oblivion. General Julian Medina's men

(Photo courtesy of Jose Cuervo)

went on a booze-fueled rampage through town, blowing things up at random, including one railway bridge. Sports fans from Oakland would continue this tradition almost a century later, after the Raiders lost Super Bowl XXXVII to the Buccaneers.

The rebels eventually won the war, and the wealth in Mexico was redistributed to some degree. As a result of media coverage of the violence in newspapers and the burgeoning film industry, tequila became known on an international level as the exotic drink of an exotic land. It was synonymous with violence, seduction, rebellion, and courage. It symbolized both justice and lawlessness. And it brought fabulous riches to La Rojena, where the Cuervos continued producing the bestselling tequila in the world.

Through the next few decades, the Cuervo company was handed down from one heir to the next. (The last guy named Jose Cuervo died in 1921.) With the exception of a few rough spots when the export market dropped off, the business continued to grow. When tequila eventually came into fashion in the States and Europe starting in the 1970s, sales went through the roof.

Today, about seventy million liters of tequila are guzzled here in the United States every year, roughly twenty-three times that of the next largest export market (which is Germany, by the way). All this drinking creates a ripple effect in the economy, lining the pockets of aspirin makers, pork taco purveyors, and plumbers on call come morning. Most of the tequila drunk here is poured into Margaritas, the bestselling cocktail in the States.

Cuervo is the oldest family-controlled liquor business in the world. Tequila is still produced at La Rojena, the oldest commercial distillery in the western hemisphere. The Cuervo family is now so wealthy they've become a secluded bunch, due to the threat of sketchy kidnap-and-ransom operations in rural Mexico. They don't get out much. People come to them.

Jose Cuervo Especial, commonly referred to as Cuervo Gold, is by far the world's bestselling single brand of tequila. But if you want to try a more authentic tequila, spend a couple extra bucks on a bottle of Cuervo Tradicional, a rich, slightly aged liquor made of 100 percent blue agave. Tradicional is a solid liquor with a tantalizing flavor and no gimmicks, just pure straightforward, high-quality tequila, similar to the stuff the first producer, Jose Antonio Cuervo, was making way back in the 1790s. Not only does the stuff taste good—the purity will save you from the morning shakes.

"Stick to Tradicional straight all night long," one Cuervo rep told me, "and you're golden the next day."

CHAPTER 9

BACARDI

EST. BIG SHOTS

Plotting to Kill Castro with the
CIA: The Inside Story of the
Planet's Bestselling Liquor

"I tell you, you make a mistake
if you don't kill him now, I tell you.
Give me the gun."
"Oh, shut up. You're drunk.
Every time you're drunk you want
to kill somebody."
—Ernest Hemingway,
To Have and Have Not

June 15, 1964. The West Wing of the White House. McGeorge Bundy, President Lyndon Johnson's savvy national security advisor, lifts a classified report up off his desk and looks it over. The document's subject: ASSASSINATION OF CASTRO. The report is signed at the bottom by government agent Gordon Chase. The document's cover letter reads:

Attached is a memorandum from the CIA describing a plot to assassinate Castro, which would involve U.S. elements of the Mafia and which would be financed by Pepin Bosch. Bosch indicated that he believes that a quick change for the better in the Cuban situation can be brought about only by the physical elimination of Fidel Castro and that his elimination is well worth $150,000. . . .

A group of assassins has agreed to carry out the plan for the $150,000, Chase's report explains. For nearly two months, the killers have been ready to execute their plan. Pepin Bosch has offered $50,000, and he is asking the U.S. government to throw in the rest of the cash, essentially to pull the trigger on the plan to bring down Washington's nemesis next door.

McGeorge Bundy leans back in his chair and takes a deep breath. He has some thinking to do. Should Washington back the plan? Could the CIA keep their involvement a secret? Can these crazy bastards pull the job off? These are tough questions, shrouded in murky variables. If there's any single thing that's cut and dry about this case, Bundy knows, it's this: Pepin Bosch has some serious balls. And it is imperative that Bosch's participation in this plot remain a highly guarded secret.

Bosch himself is no terrorist. He is the CEO of a large international liquor company—a company called Bacardi.

This scenario, recounted by Colombian investigative reporter Hernando Calvo Ospina in *Bacardi: The Hidden War* (2002), certainly sheds a new light on the liquor brand. (And it's worth noting the company's response: "No one at Bacardi believes this book is worth commenting on," said a company spokesperson.) Given the history, the antagonism should hardly seem surprising, nor unwarranted. Such was the passion for vengeance held by Pepin Bosch and other booze moguls at Bacardi. The company had been founded in Cuba almost exactly a century before and had thrived in Cuba until Castro took the island by storm on New Year's Day 1959. Castro in turn nationalized the company, usurping its Cuban assets. Bosch managed to leave with his trademark intact. He ran the international liquor operation from offices on a boat off Miami before relaunching the brand with new headquarters in the Bahamas. The Bacardi clan left the original distillery and a century's worth of history behind. The question was, for how long?

For the rest of the sixties—indeed for the rest of the twentieth century and right up until today—members of the Bacardi clan have continued to support anti-Castro causes. They have battled him with lawyers in the U.S. Supreme Court, and according to Ospina's well-researched and well-documented argument, their onetime CEO Pepin Bosch battled him by funding deadly terrorists to subvert his power—with the backing of the Central Intelligence Agency.

Starting in 1964, Pepin Bosch began supporting a group of Cuban exiles called RECE (*Representación Cubana en el Exilio*). The group was based in Miami, where, not coincidentally, Bacardi's U.S. offices are headquartered. Bosch reportedly handpicked the group's leaders himself and supported them with $10,000 monthly checks, funds that aimed to help cut down Fidel Castro. "Ostensibly, RECE was backed by the wealthy owner of the Bacardi Rum Company," according to a 1993 article that appeared in *Esquire* magazine. "But files later reviewed by congressional investigators reveal that it was really CIA supported." By the end of the sixties, RECE had been involved in so many covert operations, bombings, and other "warlike activities" against strategic targets inside Cuba that it was forced to cease operations, for a while at least. All of its men were either dead or in prison.

RECE was "one of the bloodiest terrorist organizations in the western hemisphere," Ospina writes in *Bacardi: The Hidden War.* The Cuban exile group and Bacardi "marched as one." As he also points out, Bosch later supported a group called CANF (Cuban-American National Foundation). As recently as 1990, CANF's leader, Jorge Mas Canosa (formerly a leader of RECE who had participated in Kennedy's disastrous Bay of Pigs invasion), distributed a document to high-powered leaders promising that the group's plans to remove Castro from power would come to fruition.

"Nothing nor no one will make us falter. We do not wish it but if blood has to flow, it will flow."

And yet Castro is still the man in Cuba. And Bacardi is the largest family-owned liquor company in the world, makers of the world's bestselling spirit, Bacardi rum. The Cuban Revolution was just one of the many speed bumps that rattled the company during its blistering rise to the top. Even in the early days when Bacardi was a little tin-roofed operation on the sunny island of Cuba, the company managed to survive fires in the distillery, devastating earthquakes, not to mention Cuba's brutal war for independence from Spain.

Certainly the company's founder, Don Facundo Bacardi Masso, could have had no idea of the power his name would wield and the troubles his family business would suffer when he first purchased a small distillery for 3,500 pesos in Santiago de Cuba in 1862. Back then, the original Bacardi had a simple ambition: to take the rotgut rum distilled in the islands and refine it into a gentleman's drink, a noble liquor that could rival the brandies of Europe where he was from. Bacardi had a love for liquor, and he needed to make some money to feed his children. It was that simple. Today, Bacardi sells 240 million bottles of liquor a year, ringing up nearly $3 billion in the till. Bacardi rum is a solid product across the board, especially the higher-end bottlings. But whether it can rival the brandies of Europe is anyone's guess.

Don Facundo Bacardi Masso and his brother, Jose, first moved to Santiago de Cuba in 1830 from the small town of Sitges in the Catalonia region of Spain. Fortunes were made overnight in the Caribbean. But a better future wasn't Cuba's only lure. When he first landed in Cuba in 1492, Christopher Columbus himself described the island as "the loveliest land ever beheld by human eyes." There, on the southeastern coast, the Bacardi brothers opened a store, where they sold clothes, hardware, liquor, and wine. In 1844, they registered their company—*Sociedad Facundo Bacardi y Cia*—as a clothing manufacturer.

Around this time, Don Facundo married a woman named Dona Amalia, who would become the matriarch of the Bacardi clan. Don Facundo was nearly thirty at the time. Business was good, and the couple began having children right away. At the store, the Bacardis staked their reputation on their quality products. But Don Facundo found fault in the rums that were available. Rum hadn't evolved much since Captain Henry Morgan, drunk on rumbullion, ravaged the islands two hundred years prior. It was still a rough-and-tumble drink, a liquor that left its mark. So Don Facundo started experimenting, trying to brew high-quality liquor he could sell in his store. He would get there, but it would take a while.

On August 21, 1852, tragedy struck. A massive earthquake ravaged Santiago de Cuba. A second followed days later, destroying much of the city's primitive infrastructure. It was like the earth opened up and swallowed the town whole. Fresh drinking water was contaminated with sewage, and a subsequent cholera epidemic wiped out 10 percent of Santiago de Cuba's population, including two of Don Facundo's own children. Devastated, he sailed his family back to safety in Spain. A month later, he received word from a friend still in Cuba: "If you do not return soon, I don't believe you will find anything that is yours."

The family came back to Cuba, where Don Facundo found his store in shambles, looted by desperadoes. He had to start from scratch. That was when he noticed that the Royal Spanish Development Board in Cuba was offering cash incentives for anyone who could devise modernized techniques for making good rum. He accepted the challenge.

Over the next decade, Don Facundo experimented with every step of the rum-making process, carefully refining the fiery sugarcane liquor until he became a distiller expert enough to rival any in the islands. Then, in 1862, he and his brother purchased a small distillery, a little warehouselike building on a dusty road with a tin roof and a view of swaying palm trees in the distance. The copper and cast-iron alembic still inside stood about fifteen feet high, with pipes and knobs and gauges sticking out of it. The thing looked like a primitive iron lung standing up on end.

Don Facundo began brewing Bacardi Carta Blanca, a light rum that was remarkably smooth by island standards. He also began aging sipping rums in charred casks, mellowing them the way brandies were mellowed back in Spain. (If you haven't tried the buttery Bacardi 8 neat or with a few cubes, I order you to drop this book immediately and run to your neighborhood liquor store. You will be pleasantly surprised.)

The original Bacardi was a gentleman distiller. He made "civilized rum." Early portraits of him show a thin man with brushed-back hair, light skin, and a widow's peak. With his white collar and distinguished dark jacket, he looked like a Spanish FDR.

Once his still was running, the next task was to come up with a label. The drinking clientele of Cuba was for the most part illiterate, and Don Facundo wisely figured that he would need some kind of symbol or crest for his company, something striking so drinkers could tell it apart from others. In the distillery, he and his wife noticed a bunch of fruit bats hanging from the rafters. Don Facundo's wife had studied the arts, so she knew that bats had a great significance to the history of Cuba. Native islanders regarded the swarming critters as bearers of good luck. They were thought to bring families good health. (This would make sense, since fruit bats eat mosquitos, thus helping to kill off mosquito-borne diseases.) She suggested that Don Facundo use the bat as a logo, which he did.

Bacardi rums soon became known as *El Ron del Murciélago*, or the Rum of the Bat. The graphics have changed many times over, but the bat is still the trademark that jumps off every bottle of Bacardi rum to this day.

Over the next few decades, the liquor firm managed to grow while war ravaged its homeland. But the Bacardis paid a price.

Cuba's Ten Years' War broke out in 1868. Don Facundo's son, Emilio, had taken over as company president by that time. A powerful man in the community, Emilio urged the Spanish to negotiate with Cuban rebels, who were battling for independence. The Spanish were not happy with Emilio. They came after him and arrested his father, sixty-four-year-old Don Facundo, by mistake. They later arrested Emilio in front of the distillery and shipped him off to a penal colony in North Africa.

Two years later, Emilio returned, only to watch the Bacardi distillery go up in flames. A fire broke out in the warehouse and ravaged the place. It seemed as if nothing would go right.

Still, after rebuilding the distillery with a few modern touches, the Bacardis continued brewing high-quality rum, and slowly their liquor gained popularity. Bacardi Carta Blanca rum won its first Gold Medal at a tasting in Madrid in 1877, back when that kind of thing mattered. It went on to win more medals in Paris in 1889, Chicago in 1893, Paris again in 1900, and at the St. Louis World's Fair in 1904. (Two other big liquor names also won medals at the St. Louis event: Hennessy cognac and a tiny whiskey house from Tennessee that few had ever heard of at the time, Jack Daniel's.)

In 1883, Bacardi was named official purveyor to the royal house of

Spain, a provision that allowed the company to print the royal Spanish coat of arms on their labels. Don Facundo's dream was realized; he'd turned rum into a drink for gentlemen, royalty even. In 1887, he died. But by that time, he had laid the foundation for the Bacardi empire. His sons would see the company through treacherous times to come. The company's new slogan: BACARDI: THE KING OF RUMS AND THE RUM OF KINGS.

By 1891, balance sheets showed assets of 64,839.45 pesos, nearly twenty times what Don Facundo had paid for the distillery less than thirty years earlier. And through a bizarre stroke of luck, the company was about to go international. Bombs were about to explode all over Cuba, and Bacardi sales would explode as a result.

At the end of the century, Cuba was on the verge of finally gaining its independence. In 1898, the U.S. jumped into the fray against Spain. During the three-month Spanish-American War, American troops sauntered into Cuba looking for Spanish blood and a cold drink. Together, Cuban rebels and American troops toasted Bacardi rum, mixing it with Coke (the Cuba Libre) and fruit juice. Thus America was introduced to the refreshing buzz of iced Bacardi on a hot day. U.S. troops have never left Cuba. They're still there, in Guantánamo Bay. And Bacardi in turn has never left America. As the firm would later state in its official history:

The U.S. assisted Cuba in gaining independence, and Cuba, among its many gifts in return, gave North Americans a taste for the tropical spirit made in Santiago de Cuba: Bacardi Rum.

In 1910, Bacardi opened a bottling facility in Barcelona. Four years later, the company opened a distribution center in New York. The Cuban rum brand was starting its *own* revolution. In the ensuing years, under the guidance of Don Facundo Bacardi Masso's progeny, the company would infiltrate the global spirit market. It would in effect take over the world. But not without the help of some shady characters along the way.

Like all other liquor companies in the West, Bacardi received the shock of the century in 1919, the year the U.S. government ratified the Eighteenth Amendment, outlawing booze. In the States, most liquor outfits simply collapsed. But like the emerging Seagram's em-

STIRRING IT UP

Rum is without a doubt the greatest mixing liquor around. (If you wish to argue otherwise, you clearly have no idea what you're talking about.) And of all the islands that claim centuries of delicious rum heritage, Cuba is the one that stands out as a font overflowing with amazing cocktail history. Some of the most remarkable concoctions the world has seen have sprung from the quiet island beach towns and the rowdy bars of Havana. For example . . .

CUBA LIBRE: The world's most popular cocktail was invented in Havana in 1898. During the Spanish-American War, the U.S. had allied with Cuba to fight for the little Caribbean island's independence. One day in a bar in Havana, an American captain ordered a rum and Coca-Cola on ice with a wedge of lime. Other soldiers in the bar noticed the captain sipping the peculiar drink. It was a perfect mix to cool a man off on a hot day, not to mention the fact that the drink wed the staple liquids (rum, Coke) of two nations allied in war. As the bartender passed out a round of rum and Cokes to the rest of the soldiers, the captain lifted his drink in the air and toasted: "Por Cuba Libre!" ("Free Cuba!") The Cuba Libre was born. *The mix:* Fill a highball glass with crushed ice and pour in a shot (or two) of light rum. Top off the glass with Coke, squeeze in the juice of a lime wedge, and give it a stir. Then toast once again to the freedom of Cuba.

DAIQUIRI: Bacardi executives say it was invented to enhance the delicious taste of Cuban rum. Just about everyone else says it was made to disguise the bite of crude, unrefined rum. Whichever theory you subscribe to, the story of the Daiquiri is a tasty one. In 1896, an American engineer named Jennings Cox, who was in Cuba running an iron mine, ran out of gin. The horror! A

pire in Canada, Bacardi was in a prime position to quench America's thirst—for a price.

Vacationers from the States started flocking to Cuba's white sand beaches and smoky taverns. Like Marlon Brando's character in the classic film version of *Guys and Dolls*, Americans could fly down to exotic Cuba just for a date, where they could get tipsy on Bacardi rum and dance to a little salsa music. Airplane travel had never been so easy and convenient, and adventurous folks started taking advantage of it.

"As they arrived in Havana," according to Bacardi's official history, "they were greeted at a bar that dispensed free Bacardi rum cocktails."

bespectacled fellow with a drooping, turkeylike chin, Cox considered himself a gentleman. He was expecting guests from the States, so this lack of gin sent him into a panic. He began experimenting with local ingredients until he had a drink he deemed worthy of a gentleman: rum with fresh lime juice and sugar, chilled with ice like a Martini. When his guests arrived, the drink proved a hit. He later named it after the little beach town where his iron mine was located: Daiquiri. The drink gained fame during Prohibition, when Americans flocked to Cuba to indulge in exotic Caribbean nightlife and local rum concoctions. Ernest Hemingway sealed the deal when he declared the Daiquiri his favorite cocktail during one of his sojourns in Cuba. *The mix:* Combine a shot of light rum (though two are strongly recommended), the juice of a whole lime, and a teaspoon of fine sugar. Shake with ice and strain into a cocktail glass.

MOJITO: If the Daiquiri was the drink of the pompous expatriate in Cuba, the Mojito—basically rum on ice flavored with fresh mint leaves and sugar—was the common man's drink. Originally called the Draque (after Sir Francis Drake, the fearless British explorer who sailed the Caribbean in the sixteenth century), the cocktail called for aguardiente, a harsh cane-juice liquor made by field hands. Later, it was refined with rum, and the name was changed to Mojito, after the classic Cuban cooking ingredient called mojo (a tangy marinade made with garlic and citrus). By the 1920s, the Mojito was one of the most popular drinks in Cuba, mixed in bars all over the island. *The mix:* First, muddle a small handful of fresh mint leaves with the juice of half a lime in a mixing cup using whatever tool you've got. Then toss in a good dash of bitters, a dash of simple syrup (see p.14 for the simple syrup recipe), and a shot or two of rum as you like. Shake the whole mixture and pour it all into a highball glass filled with ice.

After a few free rounds, drinkers continued downing rum, gleefully tossing their cash on bars all over the island. The word spread in the States about exotic drinks like the Daiquiri, the Mojito, the Puerto Rican–influenced Piña Colada, and plain old Rum Punch. Bacardi lured drinkers to Cuba by giving postcards to American tourists to send back to friends in the States. One such card featured a map of the Caribbean, showing Uncle Sam flying on the wing of a fruit bat from Cuba back to the U.S. The old man is giddy with drink, toasting with what looks like a silver chalice. Written across the bottom: FLYING TO HEAVEN WITH BACARDI. If you couldn't drink at home, why not take a little vacation?

Meanwhile on the American mainland, criminal gangs mapped out a route to smuggle rum in from Cuba. The rise of the Cosa Nostra during Prohibition had much to do with their links to the island. The heavily traveled seas between Cuba, Jamaica, and New Orleans became known as the "rum route." It seems hardly a coincidence that the crooked liquor baron Meyer Lansky received official permission from the Cuban government to exploit the gambling casinos on the island right when Prohibition was ending. Lansky had funneled plenty of cash into the Cuban economy during America's liquor ban. Now he was being rewarded.

While it's tough to say how much Bacardi made off the illicit liquor trade, this much is for sure: the rum company pounced on the American market the minute the booze ban was lifted in 1933. Under the guidance of Emilio Bacardi's brother-in-law, Henri Shueg, the brand continued to expand at a startling rate. And when Shueg died, his ambitious son-in-law took over, a hard-nosed guy with a taste for success, a guy with some serious balls—Jose M. "Pepin" Bosch.

Under Pepin Bosch, Bacardi moved into new headquarters in Havana, a tall palatial art deco building that symbolized the brand's triumph in the world economy. When World War II ended, as Hernando Calvo Ospina writes in *Bacardi: The Hidden War*, the rum company "was introduced into a flattened Europe almost as if it were part of the Marshall Plan. Distribution companies were started in Belgium, Switzerland, Sweden, Holland, France, Norway, Finland, and Denmark. . . . [Bacardi's] tentacles even reached Lebanon and Korea." The clan opened new distilleries in Puerto Rico, in Mexico, in Spain. No liquor company had ever attempted such radically ambitious global expansion.

And yet, as the company concentrated on internal growth, seditious activities on the island began to threaten Bacardi's stability. An underground left-wing movement had been taking root on the streets of Cuba since the early fifties, led by a bearded lawyer who could quote Marx with the best of them. Fidel Castro had begun his revolutionary career as a nonviolent protestor who worked against the dictator General Fulgencio Batista in the court system. When that failed, he organized an army and fought Batista guerrilla-style. On January 1, 1959, Castro took power.

The new dictator confiscated the Bacardi distillery and nationalized the company, seizing assets of $76 million—an unimaginable amount of money at the time. The Bacardis had a choice: fall in line with the communist regime or split. They chose the latter, and they have never forgotten what they left behind.

Remarkably, the rum company didn't falter. A global infrastructure was already in place, a huge safety net woven out of money. First the firm moved into new headquarters in the Bahamas. Then in 1972, Bacardi moved home base again to Bermuda and hired the famed architect Ludwig Mies van der Rohe (the same guy who built the Seagram Building on Park Avenue in Manhattan) to build a dramatic two-story, all-glass office building. In a sense, Bacardi became orphaned, a massive international company with no real home. Apparently, it didn't need one.

Within a decade after leaving Cuba, Bacardi became the bestselling spirit in the world, a title the brand has yet to lose.

Today, the company founded by Don Facundo Bacardi Masso sells some seventy-eight million cases of liquor a year. Bacardi rum itself is the most popular spirit brand in America. The company's liquor cabinet also includes such varied brands as Martini & Rossi (Bacardi purchased a controlling share of the wine and vermouth empire in 1992 for $1.4 billion), Dewar's (the bestselling Scotch in the U.S.), and Bombay gin. The company launched Bacardi Limon in 1995. The signature rums are brewed in distilleries in the Bahamas, India, Mexico, Panama, Trinidad, and Puerto Rico. They're bottled in plants in the U.S. (Jacksonville, Florida), Australia, Brazil, Canada, Costa Rica, Germany, Great Britain, New Zealand, Spain, and Switzerland. Many of the stockholders are descendants of Don Facundo himself. It is still very much a Bacardi-family firm.

Oddly enough, while massive booze conglomerates continue to battle each other for global domination (Bacardi is now ranked fourth, behind Diageo, Allied Domecq, and Pernod Ricard), the company's rum portfolio has been the most severely threatened in the new millennium. The culprit? Fidel Castro, once again.

In March 2001, the Cuban government shocked the booze world when it announced that Cuba would begin producing its own rum called Bacardi. Fidel Castro himself announced that the famous brand of rum "is ours and is better than theirs." Bacardi executives scrambled to block the liquor launch. The U.S. State Department backed the "real" Bacardi, forbidding Castro to follow through.

Could Castro in fact make a Bacardi rum that's better than the

Bacardi we drink now? Quite possibly, especially if it's consumed with one of those delicious cigars they wrap down there. (The combination of good rum and a Cuban cigar is sacrosanct.)

So far, Cuban Bacardi has yet to appear on shelves in bars or liquor stores anywhere in the world. But as a great man once said about Fidel Castro, "If you think you've heard the last from that bearded commie bastard, you'd better think again."

PART IV

THE SCOTS AND IRISH

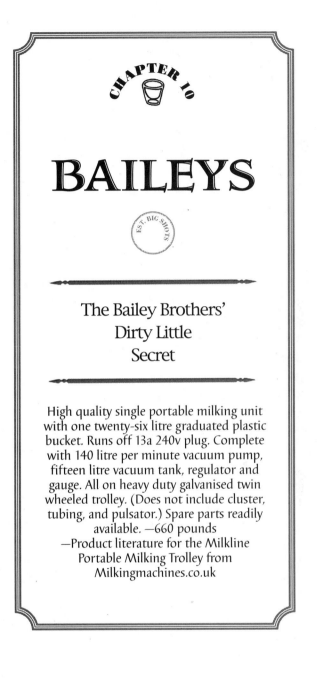

CHAPTER 10

BAILEYS

EST. BIG SHOTS

The Bailey Brothers'
Dirty Little
Secret

High quality single portable milking unit
with one twenty-six litre graduated plastic
bucket. Runs off 13a 240v plug. Complete
with 140 litre per minute vacuum pump,
fifteen litre vacuum tank, regulator and
gauge. All on heavy duty galvanised twin
wheeled trolley. (Does not include cluster,
tubing, and pulsator.) Spare parts readily
available. —660 pounds
—Product literature for the Milkline
Portable Milking Trolley from
Milkingmachines.co.uk

Whoever they are, R & A Bailey—the two guys whose names adorn the bottle of Baileys Original Irish Cream—must be a couple rich booze barons. The brand first launched in 1974, a drink completely unlike anything any barfly had ever seen before—a bizarre concoction of triple-distilled Irish whiskey, grain alcohol, sugar, vanilla, cocoa, and lots of fresh Irish dairy cream. Since then, Baileys Irish Cream has become the eighth bestselling brand of spirit on the entire planet, surpassing Jim Beam and Jose Cuervo in 2001 with sixty-six million bottles sold annually. It's the top-selling liqueur in the world, the greatest liquor brand launch in the past fifty years. So how did the Baileys pull it off? For starters, they had some pretty productive staff members.

R & A Bailey employ, oh, *forty thousand dairy cows.* Some fifty million gallons of milk go into the making of the drink every year. Divide all that teat yanking by the 1,500 dairy farmers who work for the Baileys, and you're looking at some strenuous workdays.

Stop reading for a moment and count to sixty. Done? *Two thousand glasses of Baileys have just been consumed across the globe,* a veritable river of high-calorie creamy liqueur. Today, twenty-nine years after the first bottle was uncorked in Ireland, you can walk into a bar in the Canary Islands, in the Canadian Arctic, in Zimbabwe, or in Abu Dhabi and order up a Baileys on ice. Or ten of them for that matter. (At 17 percent alcohol, one tipple is unlikely to get the job done.)

So who are the mysterious Baileys? If you look at the bottle closely, you'll see a signature at the bottom that says R & A BAILEY in clear human handwriting. If you look into the tax records in Ireland for the past three decades, you'll find no evidence of any such individual named R. or A. Bailey having paid any dues on the billions of dollars of income the drink has generated.

It's a mystery. In fact, no reporter has ever scored an interview with the Baileys, nor even laid eyes on them for that matter. Years ago, I heard a barroom story about them from a guy who claimed to be related. He said the Baileys were two bovine Irish brothers who lived on a farm in rural Ireland. They drank liquor as if it were water.

Meat pies were consumed by the dozen all day, the man said. They had all the cable movie channels imaginable and then some. In short, they were living the high life. The story sounded dubious, but who knew? I heard it from some guy in a bar, so it must be true.

Alas, after some hard-boiled detective work for the sake of this narrative, I managed to solve the riddle. The elusive Baileys do not exist.

The Bailey character is a fabrication, the brainchild of the Irish liquor executive who first whipped up the basic recipe for Irish Cream in a blender in his office: the late Mr. David Dand. The R & A stands for, well, nothing, and the signature is a fake. But there's more to this mystery, a lot more. If there ever was one, Baileys is a delicious example of what can happen when luck and some 100 proof marketing genius are mixed in a bottle and let loose upon the drinking public. It just goes to show, if it's got booze in it, people will drink anything.

The story of Baileys Original Irish Cream begins in 1970, when a company called Gilbey's Wine and Spirits moved its offices from O'Connell Street in Dublin to Naas Road. Gilbey's was a small liquor firm, but it was growing. Redbreast Irish whiskey and Gilbey's gin (very underrated for the price, by the way) were the company's big guns. But the chief executive, David Dand, a thirty-seven-year-old career liquor man with a keen eye for marketing, had paid a visit to the United States in 1961. He'd seen the drunken Smirnoff vodka revolution in action. Smirnoff sales were exploding in America. So he persuaded Smirnoff to grant Gilbey's the license to make the liquor in Ireland, the first company outside the States to do so. Not surprisingly, Gilbey's found itself in need of larger headquarters a few years later.

The Irish are still today the highest per capita Smirnoff drinkers in the world. They're also the highest per capita Baileys drinkers in the world. You'll notice a trend here.

The Naas Road plant sufficed. In fact, the place was *too* big, and David Dand decided that he should seek out some business opportunity to fill the spare space. Ideally, if he wanted to expand the company, he needed an export product to bring cash in from markets overseas. At the time, Ireland was exporting boatloads of a drink called Irish Mist (basically, whiskey and honey). Dand figured his new brand should be, like Irish Mist, uniquely Irish—a product that could use the island's "green and clean" reputation as a marketing tool while paying respect to the nation's drinking heritage.

From that moment on, tireless Gilbey's employees began working long hours, dreaming up drink recipes, and tasting them. It was brutal work. As the current head of public relations for Baileys, Peter O'Connor, notes, "every conceivable concoction you can think of" was whipped up in the office. Tariffs made importing ingredients difficult to afford en masse, so executives were left wondering what they had in their backyard besides goose dung that might make for a tempting cocktail.

"We wanted something that reflected the good things in Ireland," Dand, who died in January 1997, recalled. "It was only renowned then for the troubles in Northern Ireland. We thought agribusiness was good. Ireland was perceived as a pollution-free, wholesome country. Then we thought about whiskey. The Irish were the inventors of whiskey." Arguable.

Dand and his team cooked up the strange idea of mixing fresh cream from Ireland's dairy farms with Irish whiskey—a risky move, considering that no one had ever tried to market a cream-based liqueur. He started by literally mixing the two ingredients together in a Kenwood blender in the office. *Vroom vroom.* The outcome? "It tasted delicious."

But the mixology presented some problems. First, if you try combining cream and whiskey in a glass, you'll notice that the two separate. Second, cream rots quickly—especially when sitting on the shelf of a smoky pub. After a few days, the drink takes on the consistency of lumpy gravy.

The company began testing different combinations of cream and whiskey that'd make the drink hold tight. A team of a half dozen execs worked on it in Dublin. Dand also hired another team of scientists in London to work on the project as well. Nearly two years later, the project was complete. The scientists figured out a way to make a product that, although it was 50 percent dairy cream with no freshness additives, could be stored on a bar shelf at room temperature for over two years. (The bottle features a BEST TASTE BEFORE date on the back, the first spirit brand to do so.)

All of my attempts to coax the processing formula from company officials failed. Baileys keeps the technique "a closely guarded secret." Nevertheless, an article from the *Irish Times* back in 1995 had this to say: "To keep the product fresh, each cream molecule is coated with whiskey during the blending process when the grain spirit and chocolate and vanilla flavours are added." Now that's a mouthful. If the cream can stay preserved for that long, just think what it can do for your liver.

Once satisfied with the taste, Dand and his cronies had to come up with a brand name for their new drink. The name, the execs figured, had to be easily pronounceable in every language around the world, and it had to sound Irish—not so Irish that it would be generic, but Irish enough so the consumer could quickly identify with the drink's heritage.

The name Bailey came up right away. When the drink was still being perfected by food scientists, eager executives were calling the secret development the "Bailey Project." The scientists in England had offices across the street from the Bailey Hotel. And in Dublin, the executives would go for a pint after work at a bar called Davy Byrnes, where, from the window, they could see the sign for the competing bar across the street, the Bailey Pub. The coincidence became a topic of discussion. To boot, there's long been an association between the name Bailey and Irish dairy farmers. So Dand decided to go with the name. Perhaps the fact that there have been so many dairy farmers named Bailey would help mask the truth about the product: there was no real Bailey, and the drink is a delicious liqueur mixed with a healthy dash of marketing deceit.

Still, Dand needed a first name to bring the Bailey character to life. He turned to his company's bestselling gin, Gilbey's, which has the signature W & A GILBEY at the bottom from the two brothers, Walter and Alfred, who created it. Dand simply changed the "W" to an "R." There you have it: R & A Bailey.

Launch night. November 26, 1974. A small crowd of invited guests gathered at Tailors Hall in Dublin to taste a new drink that was about to be shipped to pubs and stores throughout Ireland. It was a dramatic choice of venue for a little party: the oldest surviving guild hall in Dublin, set in the heart of the city in the shadow of the towering Christ Church Cathedral, where Handel's *Messiah* was first performed. The old redbrick hall had hitherto hosted meetings of the utmost importance to the political and economic history of Ireland. Guests were wondering exactly what was in store for them that night.

Baileys production director Tom Murray brought the first couple cases from the office on Naas Road by car to Tailors Hall. The product was basically improvised, an ad hoc Baileys label stuck on a Redbreast whiskey bottle full of a stuff called "Irish Cream." It was a twenty-minute drive to the Hall, and Murray worried that the drink would separate on the way over. It didn't.

As he greeted fellow drinkers and members of the press, he poured the liqueur into glasses. It had the color and consistency of coffee mixed with whipping cream. When swirled, the thick liquid clung to the sides of the glass and gave off an odor more chocolate than alcohol. Curious drinkers stared at it warily and sipped it with furrowed brows.

At the time, the Irish were still mostly a whiskey-and-Guinness crowd, with vodka cocktails just catching on in a big way. A sweet cream didn't exactly impress their taste buds. After four years of development and an estimated $55,000 of initial investment, the response to the tasting that night was hardly what David Dand and his scientists had hoped for. As one account of the evening went, "Suffice to say that many left the launch party discreetly and headed for the Lord Edward for a '*real drink.*'"

Nevertheless, cases of Baileys were shipped to outlets throughout Ireland some days later. Company spokesmen followed to organize tastings similar to the one at Tailors Hall. The marketing strategy aimed to make the consumer think he had stumbled onto an authentic Irish drink that had been around in the countryside for centuries. (Thus the bottle was designed in the shape of an old whiskey jug.) The first year, daring drinkers around the country sucked down eight thousand cases of the stuff—a decent showing. (Today the company produces twice that much Baileys *every day.*) But overseas, the response was poor, to say the least.

Dand traveled to the States to visit importers, with the country's enormous Irish-American population in mind. The trip didn't go so well.

"Jesus, David," one importer said after tasting Baileys, "this shit? It'll *never* sell." Apparently, the American market wasn't ready for the stuff.

The tasting campaign continued in Ireland for three years, and by 1978, Dand finally began to see some results. At home, sales started to take off. The company exported some six hundred thousand cases that year to markets in Holland, Great Britain, and Denmark. Then, year by year, sales began to snowball. More and more drinkers took to the taste of the strange liqueur—particularly women. Money

The late David Dand, chairman and managing director of R&A Bailey & Co. Ltd. *(Image courtesy of R&A Bailey Ltd.)*

started pouring in. Suddenly, one day, shocked executives found that their chart graphs no longer fit on the tackboard.

By 1980, consumers in six countries guzzled 1.45 million cases of Baileys—a shocking number, well beyond market expectations. If you lined all those bottles up in one place, they'd be roughly equivalent to the length of the smile on David Dand's face.

In Australia in particular, the launch was spectacular. Dand met there with a distributor who imported four hundred cases to see if it would sell. Days later, retailers in Australia were hanging signs in their windows advertising new shipments of the drink on the way. One example:

BAILEYS ARRIVING TOMORROW.
AUCTION AT 3 O'CLOCK.

SMELLS LIKE CREAM SPIRIT

Baileys by itself? *Yawn.* Poured into a pint of Guinness with a dash of whiskey and guzzled? That's more like it.

🥃 **CEMENT MIXER:** One ounce of Baileys in a shot glass topped (carefully, so the liquids layer) with lime juice. Shoot it. Then mix it in your mouth before swallowing.

🥃 **BAILEYS COMET:** A half shot of Baileys, a third of a shot of dark crème de cacao, and a third of a shot of vodka, splash of half and half, splash of soda. Shake with ice and strain into a cocktail glass.

🥃 **IRISH CAR BOMB:** A shot glass filled half with Baileys and half with Irish whiskey dropped into a pint of Guinness and guzzled. *Ka-boom!*

🥃 **BLOW JOB:** Equal parts Kahlua, Baileys, and vodka in a shot glass, topped with a dollop of whipped cream. Must be gulped down in one go—without using your hands.

🥃 **IRISH COFFEE:** Hot black coffee with a half shot each of Baileys and Irish whiskey dumped in. Top with whipped cream if you're feeling silly.

🥃 **AFTER FIVE:** A half shot of peppermint schnapps, plus a shot of Baileys layered on top in a rocks glass.

At the plant where the product is produced in Dublin, trucks arrived from farms in the countryside incessantly with huge tanks full of fresh cream, and the processing took no time. The cream was quickly separated from the milk, tested for quality control, and mixed with the other ingredients that very day. The company paid a nearby distiller to make the triple pot stilled blended Irish whiskey, aged four to five years. The "finest Irish spirit" (pure and straight grain alcohol) came from County Cork in the southwest. The only two imported ingredients—cocoa from West Africa and vanilla from Madagascar—arrived in liquid form for easy mixing.

Once processed, the product didn't need any aging, so it could be shipped right away with no warehousing costs. The stuff was bottled and ready to drink within thirty-six hours of the moment the cream arrived at the plant. By contrast, the whiskey distillers down the road

BRAIN HEMORRHAGE: One shot of Baileys and half a shot of strawberry schnapps layered in a rocks glass and topped with a couple drops of grenadine (to simulate the blood, you see).

MUDSLIDE: A half shot of Kahlua, a half shot of Baileys, a half shot of vodka, layered in that order in a rocks glass. To make it frozen, add a scoop of vanilla ice cream and some Oreo cookies. Then blend it all up and serve it in a large glass of your choice with a dollop of whipped cream.

COCAINE LADY: A third of a shot each of light rum, vodka, Kahlua, Baileys, and light cream. Mix it all and pour over ice in a highball glass with a dash of cola on top.

BUTTER BALL: Two-thirds of a shot of butterscotch schnapps (eek) and a third of a shot of Baileys layered in a shot glass.

B-52: Two-thirds of a shot each of Kahlua, Baileys, and Grand Marnier layered in that order in a rocks glass.

ALMOND JOY: A third of a shot each of Baileys, Kahlua, amaretto, and vodka shaken with ice, dumped into a highball glass, and topped with a dash of fresh cream.

might hold on to their liquor for a decade before they could make a penny.

Finally, in the early eighties, David Dand convinced an American importer to take a chance on Baileys. The importer requested twenty-five thousand cases. Dand refused. He wanted his brand launched nationally in the States—all or nothing. "I went for it hell for leather," he was known to say about the sweet success of his liqueur. He convinced the importer to take seventy-five thousand cases. As it turned out, the launch in America was successful beyond Dand's wildest dreams. Boozers in this country drank *125,000 cases* that very first year.

Today, David Dand's brainchild sells 5.2 million cases annually. If you were to ask any of the tasters at the original launch party at Tailors

Hall in Dublin back in 1974, they'd tell you that five million cases is about 4.9 million more than anyone would've expected.

The drink's available in 130 different countries. Roughly 30 percent of the sales go down right here in the United States, making us ever so slightly fatter than we used to be. Since 1978, companies have launched imitation cream liqueurs all over the world, concoctions that mix cream with wine, wild fruits, bananas, brandy. Ireland alone produces Emmet Cream Liqueur, Ashbourne, Carolans, and St. Brendan's. But Baileys Original Irish Cream still holds 50 percent of the global market.

The liquor powerhouse Diageo now owns the brand. (Diageo also owns Johnnie Walker, Guinness, Tanqueray, Smirnoff, Captain Morgan, Cuervo, J&B Scotch, etc. You'll need a couple aspirin after just *imagining* what company picnics are like.) Diageo expects sales of Baileys to double to ten million cases per year possibly by 2005. Growing sales are spurred by the barrels of dough the company is pouring into advertising what it calls "the brand essence": sensuousness, indulgence, togetherness.

Chances are, if you consider yourself at least one of these three things—sensuous, indulgent, or together—you probably have a bottle of Baileys in your home. And if you don't, you'll probably be getting one for Christmas this year, hopefully along with a copy of this book. (More than a quarter of the total Baileys sales occur during Christmas week.)

Maybe while you sip a glass, you can dream up some kind of beverage that you can mix at home in your own blender—a combination of things that, until you taste it, you wouldn't dream of putting together in the same glass. Maybe you can market your drink and make billions. Apparently, you just never know.

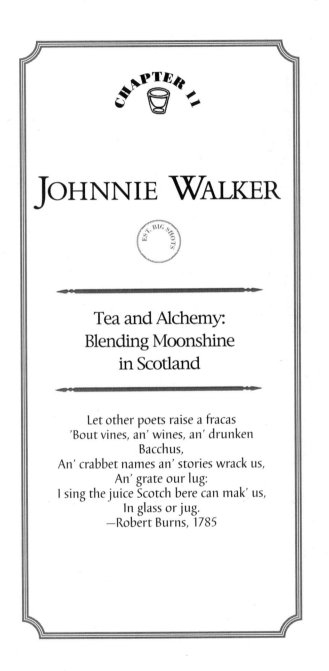

CHAPTER 11

JOHNNIE WALKER

EST. BIG SHOTS

Tea and Alchemy:
Blending Moonshine
in Scotland

Let other poets raise a fracas
'Bout vines, an' wines, an' drunken
Bacchus,
An' crabbet names an' stories wrack us,
An' grate our lug:
I sing the juice Scotch bere can mak' us,
In glass or jug.
—Robert Burns, 1785

The year was 1820. Just fifteen years old, a boy named John Walker arrived for his first day of work at a little store in the town of Kilmarnock, Scotland. Some time before, the boy's father had died unexpectedly, and a life insurance policy coughed up £417, just enough to purchase a 7 Eleven–style store that John could run with his mother. The shop was set in a yellow building right on a thoroughfare in town, with a big front window and a welcoming wooden door. On sale: groceries, a variety of teas, and a selection of single-malt whiskies from the distilleries that marked the countryside in the north. Aside from the sign above the door—JOHN WALKER—there was nothing to distinguish the shop from any other.

Jump forward nearly two centuries. That same John Walker's name is printed on the label of the bestselling international brand of whiskey in history. The words ESTABLISHED 1820 on the bottle mark the date when the fifteen-year-old first stepped foot in his store in Kilmarnock. A likeness of Walker as an older gentleman—walking, appropriately—is printed on the bottom of the bottle, the trademark "Striding Man." If you stumble into any civilized bar in the world today, on any continent, the bartender will know Johnnie Walker's name before that of the president of his own country.

Now consider the fact that John Walker himself never distilled a commercial whiskey in his life. He started out as the equivalent of Apu on *The Simpsons*, running a shop day to day, stocking the shelves. So how did he pull off such startling success? Walker had an idea, a simple thought he might've stumbled on to while taking his monthly bath one evening. As ideas go, it was a good one. That simple idea helped evolve the crude and unpredictable Scotch whiskey of the early years into the smooth velvety stuff we drink today, and made a lot of people a lot of money, Johnnie Walker included.

But like most other liquor barons, Johnnie Walker's story isn't just about liquor. His success story paints a portrait of an entire people in a place in time, a slice of history in a profoundly twisted era. During the original Walker's life, whiskey wasn't just a drink—it was a national currency, a lucrative resource caught up in the conflict between the Scots and the English (somewhat in the same way that slavery would come to be in the States a few years later). The story of Johnnie Walker is a story about illegal distillers, smugglers, riots, tax men, and violence—not to mention drunkenness.

In order to understand who Johnnie Walker was and what he accomplished, you have to start with the story of Scotch whiskey itself—hardly a boring tale, especially if you have a taste for the stuff. The Scottish originally inherited the art of distillation from Christian monks. Some say it was around A.D. 1200. Others say A.D. 500. The monks imparted this wisdom while spreading the news that the bearded Son of God—the Lord Jesus Christ Almighty—had been born to a virgin in Israel, had walked on water, had been nailed to a cross, and had risen again only to disappear like a vapor. (Which news was more important to the future of humankind—the discovery of distillation or the coming of the savior—is anyone's guess.)

The Scots grew barley, and they were already using the "ménage à trois" of barley, yeast (which grew naturally on the barley), and water to brew beer. When distilled, beer turned into whiskey.

During the Dark Ages, liquor was used mainly for medicinal purposes. The Scots, who spoke a form of Gaelic, called their booze *usquebaugh*—"water of life." When mixed with herbs, oils, sugar, and spices, the distillate was used to cure the sick and ward off diseases like smallpox and the black death. If you were on your deathbed, that was pretty much all the medicine a "doctor" could offer you. And maybe an enema, if you were so inclined.

As time passed, farmers became the major distillers—only natural, considering that they grew barley to feed sheep. Whatever was left over, they used to make whiskey that they could sip and sell to purveyors in town. Gradually liquor became a staple part of the Scottish diet. It was used, and still is used, to bless the region's signature dish: haggis (sheep stomach stuffed with barley and minced organ meat—an extraordinarily underrated meal . . . no joke). A shot was poured over the top of a steaming plate just before it was devoured.

As Dr. Johnson wrote in the first English Dictionary in 1755, fifty years before John Walker's birth, "usquebaugh" was . . .

    . . . a compound distilled spirit, being drawn on aromaticks; and the Irish sort is particularly distinguished

for its pleasant and mild flavor. The Highland sort is somewhat hotter; and by corruption in Scottish [i.e., from the
Gaelic to the Scottish form of English] they call it
whisky.

At the time, the Scots and the English had a love/hate relationship.
They had been going at it like a couple bitch-slapping stepsisters. The
English were beginning to build a massive empire, colonizing the Far
East, Africa, and America. The government in London fancied Scotland as well. The Scottish wanted independence, and they were inclined to fight. Like oil in the Middle East, the "water of life" was a
resource that got tangled in the fray.

On January 31, 1644, the Scottish government imposed a tax on
whiskey (two shillings eight pence per Scottish pint, which is about
two liters) to raise money for war. "On everie pynt of aquavytie ['water of life' in mutant Latin] or strong watter is sold within the coun-
trey," a tax was levied to support "an armie to be sent into England."

As we know now, the tax wasn't enough. The Scots lost their battle and were quickly made to bend to the whims of the English
monarchy. Restrictions were placed on the meeting of Scottish clans,
on the wearing of kilts, on the shouting of the word "eh," and other
traditions. More important, the English sent in an army of tax men to
try to collect money from whiskey distillers in the north.

Whiskey was money. As one contemporary Scottish minister put
it: "Distilling is almost the only method of converting our victual into
cash for payment of rent and servants and whisky may in fact be called
our staple commodity." Surely the distillers in the countryside weren't
going to pay out some of their hard-earned money to the wealthy English monarchy, especially when they could barely afford to feed their
children. They would continue making whiskey, but they would hide
the production from the taxman. Thus began the great tradition of illicit distilling and midnight smuggling runs.

As Helen Arthur describes in *Whisky: The Water of Life*:

The tax collector would be accompanied by English soldiers who offered some form of protection. The soldiers
were called "redcoats," named for the color of their uni-
forms. Outwitting the redcoats became a national sport in

Scotland and tales of heroism and cunning against them are woven into the history of individual distilleries.

Unlike today's massive operations, these distilleries were small makeshift jobs. The illegal still was made out of a big metal pot used to boil a fermentation over a big fire. The tax collectors would wait on a hill somewhere and search for a spiral of smoke rising, which would tip them off. Then they'd simply follow the trail of smoke right to the fire. (Think of cops in the new millennium hunting for crystal-meth labs in the desert.)

The tax man made about £50 a year. But if one had the luck to capture a smuggler, he'd get *an extra year's pay*, plus half of the loot, which might have been a lifetime's worth of liquor! There was plenty of incentive on both sides. But usually, by the time the tax man arrived at the source of the smoke, the entire still would have been disassembled, and the distillers would be hightailing it through the countryside in a horse-drawn carriage with jugs of hard stuff sloshing around in the back.

The underground distillers brought their whiskey to a middleman, what they called a "bletherman" (which meant someone who chatters nonsense). This way, the distillers never made contact with the real purchasers, the men who would be selling the whiskey to the general public, in shops that lined the streets of every city and town.

One such shopkeeper was a young Johnnie Walker, who sold these whiskies in his store in Kilmarnock.

During Johnnie Walker's very first year in business, the English made more than fourteen thousand raids on illegal distillers in the north. The entire whiskey industry was fueled by toothless moonshiners carting around rusty stills—hardly a reliable lot.

The biggest casualty was the whiskey itself, which is where Johnnie Walker comes in. The batches that made it to Walker's stock were all single malts, harsh on the tongue, with potent flavors that varied from jug to jug. Most of the privileged class, Walker's desired clientele, didn't bother with the stuff. It simply didn't taste good. Instead, they drank the fine wines and cognacs guys like Richard Hennessy were shipping in from France with more frequency and at increasingly cheaper prices.

So how could a shop owner get rid of his single malts and make a profit? Turning the lousy juice on the shelves into fine whiskey would be like spinning yarn into gold. But Johnnie Walker had an idea. Some might argue that Walker inherited the idea, which is entirely possible. Nevertheless . . .

One of Walker's tasks at his shop was to blend teas. Tea was imported into Scotland from all over the world—most notably the Far East—on ships called tea clippers. (One such boat was the *Cutty Sark*. Today's Scotch of the same name points to the interwoven histories of these two drinks.) The tea craze had grabbed hold of England and Scotland the century before Walker's time, never to let go, and the blending of the different dried leaves from around the globe was considered an art form. If done well, the whole of a blended tea would taste better than the sum of its parts. The blend would bring out the different flavors, add sugar to spice, lend subtlety to bitterness. If a purveyor was good at blending, he could make some dough.

So why couldn't the same principle be used to blend a consistent whiskey out of a variety of sketchy single malts? With this in mind, Johnnie Walker began mixing different crude whiskies. He noticed that, as with tea, he could use the different ingredients to make a product that delivered a consistent taste. The mixture could also lend the liquor a depth of flavor and refinement, bring out different hints of flavor and a longer, more satisfying finish. Various concoctions could favor unique flavor aspects—smoke, honey, fruit—which could be marketed to particular customers with big wallets.

As Walker aged, so did his preferred blended whiskies, which began to draw sums of money. Lines formed at the shop in Kilmarnock. Valued customers placed private orders for exclusive blends. As Walker's fame grew, so did his business.

A few other whiskey purveyors got into blending back in the mid-nineteenth century, and some of the brands are still major labels today: Teacher's, Chivas, Cutty Sark. Today, 95 percent of the whiskey sold around the planet is blended whiskey.

Johnnie Walker died on October 19, 1857. Fortuitously, Walker was blessed with pretty astute progeny. With the help of a couple of amazing coincidences, his son and grandsons would turn a well-regarded blend of single malts into the first internationally recognizable brand of liquor.

Johnnie's son, Alexander Walker, was twenty years old when he inherited the business. The younger Walker was not only a master blender like his father, but he possessed a marketing mind way ahead of his time. It was almost as if a genie had popped out of a bottle of whiskey one day and told him that the world would soon become obsessed with advertising and marketing.

Alexander created a new blend that he named Old Highland Whisky. Then he put his mind to branding it. He knew he wanted some subtle gimmick that would set the liquor apart from the heady competition. So he conjured up the square bottle with the signature slanted black label that Johnnie Walker still uses today. The first copyright was registered in 1867. The Walker company's motto was "to make our whisky of such a quality that nothing in the market shall come before it."

At this time, the cognac market collapsed, and the tragedy played into Alexander Walker's favor. An outbreak of phylloxera—a bug that eats grapevines—took France by storm in 1863. The little grubworms followed the British army's example and devastated the nation with apparent ease. As they watched their livelihoods disappear, French winemakers did everything they could to stop the marauding bugs. Particularly, they buried live toads in the roots of each vine. A great idea! It didn't work. Wine and cognac production plummeted, and folks in Scotland and England accustomed to the finer flavors turned their tongues to the local market.

Meanwhile, the railway system was making commerce easier and more lucrative than it had ever been. During the original Johnnie Walker's life, 1.5 million tons of British iron were laid out in tracks across the Isles, just in time to help Alexander Walker. Suddenly, a case of bottled whiskey could be carried overnight to Edinburgh, Glasgow, or London. It could be taken to ports and shipped all over the world. The audience for Johnnie Walker's blended whiskey grew exponentially, and the business went through the proverbial roof.

Alexander Walker died a rich man in 1889. His two sons took over and made the final moves that turned the blend of single malts customers bought in Johnnie Walker's shop into the brand we know today. Alexander Junior was the blender, with the skill to continue improving the whiskey's quality. He had a taste for the stuff produced in Cardhu in the heart of Speyside, so he invested in a distillery there that remains the cornerstone of the Johnnie Walker stable.

The other son, George Paterson Walker, was the marketer. One day, George invited the famous cartoonist Tom Browne to lunch, and the two men discussed the label. As George later remembered:

THE JOHNNIE WALKER CATALOG

If you head into a bar and ask for Johnnie Walker, the bartender will probably respond with a question: "Red or black?" And if you're in a high-end joint, perhaps with a piano man feigning Cole Porter and a whore peddling a four-digit figure, the bartender might add to the list, "Red, black, gold, or blue?" Herewith the particulars on Johnnie Walker's stable of whiskies.

RED LABEL: Launched in 1909, this Scotch is a blend of roughly thirty-five single malts of varied ages. It's the single most popular whiskey in the world. As far as character goes, Red Label has plenty (sweet and smoky, with a rich amber hue), but not in comparison to other Walker whiskies. If you're aiming to mix Scotch with soda or whatever, this is a good pick.

BLACK LABEL: The original branded Johnnie Walker whiskey hit shelves back in 1867. A rich concoction of forty single malts, all of them aged at least twelve years, it has a full flavored character with hints of raisin, orange zest, and peat smoke. As far as blended whiskies go, this is a classic. Even if you don't like the stuff, you should have some on hand, just so you can stare at the gorgeous bottle.

In supplying an old photograph of my grandfather [Johnnie Walker] to the late Tom Browne, artist, he drew a small figure quickly, copying my grandfather's face and style, which was so attractive that we decided it would be most effective, and from this small figure of about one inch in height the whole of the advertising has gradually evolved.

The "Striding Man"—one of the world's first globally recognized advertising icons—was born. The ad worked like a charm, and today you can still see that same man striding off billboards and bottles all over the world. By 1920, Johnnie Walker was on the top shelf of bars in 120 countries. Thirteen years later, the company was given a royal warrant to supply whiskey to Britain's King George V. Johnnie Walker is still the official purveyor of whiskey to the British monarchy today.

In the mood for a wee dram? Try your hand with a bottle of Black Label, the company's original branded whiskey and a benchmark among blended Scotches. When swirled neat in a nosing glass, the

GOLD LABEL: This whiskey's made partly with single malt from the Clynelish distillery in the northern Highlands of Scotland. The water source is near the Kildonan Hills, the site of the 1848 gold rush. You can still pan for gold there today. Gold Label's made from an exclusive selection of fifteen whiskies, all aged at least eighteen years. Flecked with honeyed spice, structured by a creamy character, it's the buttered scone of blended whiskies and, in my humble opinion, the finest of the Johnnie Walker stable.

BLUE LABEL: I first tasted this blend at a cigar bar called Match in Soho in Manhattan. The bartender happened to be my roommate at the time. Not only was Match the only place I could afford to drink back then, but it was a bar where I could line up five costly whiskies and taste test them. Among the blends, and with the exception of Gold Label, which they didn't have, Johnnie Walker Blue Label won mé over, beating the much cheaper Ballantine's by a nose hair. A profound whiskey with the complex character of a nineteenth-century blend (hints of smoke, toasted nuts, citrus, even seaweed), some of the whiskey inside a bottle of Blue Label might be a hundred years old. Whether it's worth the scary price tag is anyone's guess.

syrupy Scotch clings to the side, the legs drizzling slowly. A sniff reveals a mystery of peat smoke, chocolate, and berry. When you're satisfied, raise the glass in honor of a simple shop owner, dead and gone now for nearly two centuries, and have a sip. When the glass is empty, rinse and repeat as necessary.

PART V
TOP SHELF

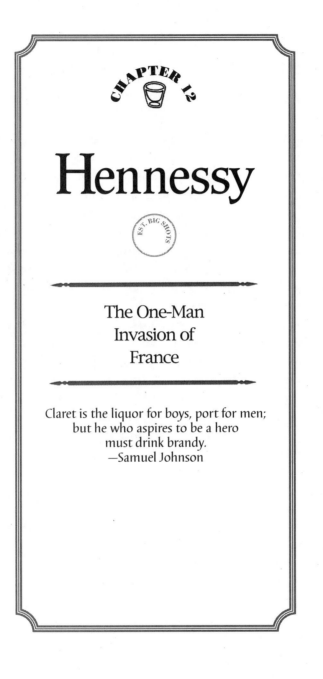

CHAPTER 12

Hennessy

EST. BIG SHOTS

The One-Man
Invasion of
France

Claret is the liquor for boys, port for men;
but he who aspires to be a hero
must drink brandy.
—Samuel Johnson

Richard Hennessy—founder of the largest cognac firm on the planet—started his company way back in 1765. And yet, though the company saw remarkable success throughout the centuries, Hennessy sales skyrocketed as never before just this past decade. In the late 1990s, sales were growing 10 percent annually in the U.S., which is today the world's largest cognac market. In part, the renewed taste for this particular brandy (as well as high-end wine, for that matter) was a function of the new refined palate among young people in this country, many of whom can now pronounce words like "cornichon" and "tagliatelle."

And yet the oddest pocket of new cognac drinkers crystallized in the inner city starting in the eighties, where status-conscious gangsters began drinking it as a display of wealth, which translated to power on the street. "Black smack" or "C and C"—meaning cognac and cocaine—caught on as a favorite combo in tough neighborhoods in New York, Houston, Detroit, and L.A. Street boozers were guzzling so much cognac, Courvoisier marketed a bottle specifically designed to fit in a hip pocket.

One could only imagine the original Richard Hennessy—founder of the Hennessy firm, clad in his eighteenth-century frock coat, tights, and frilly cravat—chatting about his liquor on a street corner with Tupac Shakur, who, before he was gunned down in 1996 in Las Vegas, became a walking Hennessy advertisement.

"Fuck friends, 'cause when in danger those niggas change," Tupac would chant.

"Pardon, sir?"

"Puff weed, and stuff G's in my sock, G! Call Ki's and Hennessy where tha Glock be!"

Then Tupac would yank a flask from his pocket.

"I'd love a tipple," Richard Hennessy would say, scratching his white wig nervously.

Alas, the two were never destined to meet. They were separated by a couple centuries' worth of brandy drinkers. But both lived remarkably lives, with great ambition fueled by fine cognac, among other things. Like Tupac's, Richard Hennessy's life was full of everything that makes for a fascinating profile: liquor, money, power, violence, and more liquor. Though his life story is hardly as intoxicating as the brandy he made, the two go pretty well together, if you get the point.

The first thing you should know about Richard Hennessy: he was an Irishman of English descent. Now this is remarkable, given the fact that he made his riches by producing French liquor in France and selling most of it at great profit outside of France.

You'll remember that, for centuries up until recently, and to some degree still today, the English and the French have hated each other. The French, who can be notably jingoistic about the finer points of their culture, take great pride in their cognac, which is regarded by many liquor experts to be the finest spirit ever distilled. And the English? "Up your ass, you bastard" is a common London phrase used in regard to England's neighboring foe. The Brits are quick to point out that, according to recent studies, 40 percent of Frenchmen don't change their underwear every day. But if a Brit *really* wants to take the piss out of a Frenchman, he can always fall back on France's troubling cognac enigma.

If one were to honor Great Britain's greatest conqueror of France, it might just be Captain Richard Hennessy, a soldier of fortune who sailed with the Irish Brigade as a young man, only to end up one of the greatest liquor barons in French history. Don't misunderstand: he was well loved in France, even when that nation was at war with his own. This was all part of his mastery.

Hennessy landed in France by happenstance. When he was barely twenty, this son of a lord sailed from his home in County Cork in Ireland to serve as a military captain for France's Henry XV for a good wage. Hennessy fought in Fontenoy in 1745, where he was wounded; in Flanders in forty-six; in Cherbourg in forty-eight. He'd fight anyone, as long as there was a paycheck waiting.

Hennessy ended up garrisoned on the French island Île de Re, where he fell in love with the country's spectacular Atlantic coast. There, numerous rivers dump into the ocean, and the marshy coast is speckled with medieval villages hugging the sea. Just north of Bordeaux, the river Charente greets the Atlantic. Up the Charente a short distance, Hennessy found a small town, population five thousand people, called Cognac.

By this time, Cognac already had a reputation for its *eaux-de-vie* ("water of life"). Now get this straight right off, lest you get kicked out of your local cigar bar: all cognac is brandy, but not all brandy is cognac. Only brandy made in Cognac can be called cognac (just like sparkling wine made anywhere but Champagne is not champagne, but "sparkling wine"). Brandy is, quite simply, wine distilled into liquor, and it was almost certainly the first liquor ever made. (Today, most manufacturers add caramel for color and a dash of sugar to mellow the flavor.) The Dutch were the first to form a taste for it. They called the libation *brandywijn*—literally "burned wine"—and thus the name brandy. To make the stuff, they imported wine from France for distilling. By Hennessy's time, the French had started making brandy themselves. They could clear a bigger profit that way. Instead of shipping hundreds of casks of wine, they could distill it themselves into a higher proof beverage, making it easier to ship in smaller, more concentrated quantities. For this reason, they made the brandy fairly strong—up to 70 percent alcohol (today, by law, it cannot exceed 45 percent). Drinkers then diluted it with water. Or not.

Richard Hennessy was thirty-six when he set up shop. Originally, he stopped in Bordeaux, but he quickly moved to Cognac because, as he said, "it was the only town in the province with a market dealing in brandy." Of all the towns in France, or anywhere for that matter, Cognac had everything a guy could need to create a perfect liquor from grapes. Porous soil rich in chalk. A seasonal climate with plenty of rain and sun. "No other region can produce cognac," wrote the eminent French historian Professor Louis Ravaz in 1900. "The slightest difference in the climate, the soil, and so on is enough to change completely the nature of the brandy." In addition, the river Charente that split the town had a bottom deep enough for large boats and provided a clear path to the Atlantic, perfect for shipping. (The Cognacais had been exporting salt for years before they discovered the art of distilling.)

Hennessy began exporting cognac just for fun. And he wanted his friends in Ireland and England to have a taste. In this ultraquaint rustic village, he made his home among the tiny cobblestone streets and sixteenth-century chateaux. Some of the cognac names familiar to today's drinkers were already hawking liquor at the time, Delamain and Martell in particular. Like them, Hennessy began buying brandies from the local grape growers, who were distilling the stuff themselves, and blending them for a complex and long-lasting flavor.

It was already common knowledge that the longer the brandy aged in wood casks, the finer and mellower the flavor. From the still, the so-called burned wine resembled grappa; it was clear and fiery. To give it its flavor and color, one needed to age it in casks, in a cellar where it was cool and protected from the sun's rays. Hennessy searched for ten years before finding the perfect spot for his Founder's Cellar, on the right bank of the river Charente. There he blended the brandies he bought from vintners throughout the region and aged them in oak barrels, the so-called "sleeping beauties," as one contemporary called the casks. (Visitors to Cognac today can tour this very same cellar, home of the most famous collection of brandies in the world, where casks as old as the U.S. Constitution lie waiting to be tapped.)

Hennessy was aging most cognacs for no more than a year, though some as long as four years. Price was set by age as well as the precise geographic region in Cognac where the grapes were grown. (Some are considered better than others.) When the liquor had matured, it was sold in anonymous casks, which were then bottled and labeled by the importing companies in those particular cities where they were to be drunk. In other words, the average consumer didn't have any idea who Richard Hennessy was. Just as well. The growing clientele he enjoyed was drinking the liquor in part because of its French mystique. If the French are experts at anything, it is food and drink. But Hennessy wasn't French at all.

Oddly enough, the people of Cognac didn't drink a lot of their native liquor. In Richard Hennessy's time, most of the brandy made in the region was exported to England, Holland, Ireland, and Denmark. Actually, Hennessy thought it would be vulgar to sell his liquor to the locals. He preferred to sell it abroad.

At first, as Richard's grandson Auguste later noted, "The fact is that the public originally took to drinking brandy and water for medicinal reasons, and having found it both pleasant and effective, they are likely to continue." During the 1770s, the café society of London developed a taste for luxe libations including sherry, port, and "coniack brandy." French liquor became a symbol of decadence and wealth, the same way it would centuries later for street thugs like Tupac and Snoop Dogg.

Being an Irishman of English blood and the son of a lord to boot,

MAKING THE GRADE

Those weird acronyms on cognac labels? They actually mean something. Back in 1865, when Maurice Hennessy (Richard Hennessy's grandson) started bottling cognac, he created a classification system to help drinkers know what they were getting into. The system was eventually picked up by other brands, so it's now industry-wide. Here's how it works:

♉ **VS:** Very Superior (also known as Three Star). The VS is a blend of brandies, the youngest of which is at least 2.5 years old. If

Hennessy had great connections among London importers. He was also an experienced sea captain, so he had a leg up in the shipping business. Within a few years, Hennessy was the largest cognac merchant in the world, rivaling Martell, a close second. The two emerged as a duopoly, locked in a spirited competition that basically controlled the market. All was well. And drunk.

Then came the French Revolution. One would think that a rich foreigner running a lucrative business would have a tough time keeping his head on straight when the poor masses rebelled and guillotined France's King Louis XVI and any other rich folk they could get their hands on. *Au contraire*. While many of the cognac merchants suffered during the Revolution, Richard Hennessy made out splendidly. Though quite rich, he was not considered bourgeois. As an Irish refugee from British yoke, Richard was celebrated as Citizen Hennessy, a man of the people. Though it's tough to prove today, it seems likely that Hennessy profited by selling his liquor to the revolutionaries.

At the end of the eighteenth century, business was continuing to grow. During the French-English wars, Hennessy wisely shipped his cargo to London through neutral ports. As French and English citizens murdered each other in droves, the brandy merchant continued selling his cognac from France to the Brits, keeping his highbrow clientele numb and happy. He also made the first sale of cognac to America in 1794, to one Jacob Schieffelin, who ran a small apothecary shop on Maiden Lane in lower Manhattan. (Schieffelin's descendants have represented Hennessy cognac in this country ever since; today, Moët-

you're into mixing your cognac cocktail-style—say, a brandy and ginger ale—this is the stuff.

 VSOP: Very Superior Old Pale (otherwise known as VO and Reserve). This cognac's a blend of brandies, the youngest of which is at least 4.5 years old.

 XO: Extra Old (the same as Napoleon, Extra, and Hors d'Age). A high-end cognac for real enthusiasts; each of the brandies in the blend is at least six years old.

Hennessy–Louis Vuitton and Diageo jointly own the highly regarded importing company Schieffelin & Somerset, which is based in New York.)

As the eighteenth century came to a close, the region of Cognac was pumping out nearly two million gallons of brandy annually. It came to be a topic of discussion, this delicious liquor. Thus the famous quote from the French politician Talleyrand, a contemporary of Richard Hennessy's, on how to drink the stuff: "You take your glass in the hollow of your hand, you warm it, you rotate it with a circular movement so that the spirit gives off its aroma. Then you carry it to your nostrils and inhale . . . and then, my dear sir, you put down your glass and talk about it."

Cognac's reputation was made.

Richard Hennessy died in 1800, at the age of eighty. But there were other Hennessys to come, men who would carry on the tradition of making stellar brandy all the way to the present day: James Sr., James Jr., Auguste, two Maurices, and a Gilles. (Of course, there had to be a Gilles.)

There were a few rough spots over the years. An outbreak of phylloxera nearly destroyed the entire industry at the end of the nineteenth century. Cognac supplies plummeted, sending prices through the roof, so only the wealthy could afford it. This reinforced the drink's wealthy fan base, which it still enjoys today. Cognac producers also battled fraud, as shady moonshiners all over Europe began distilling rotgut and selling it as "cognac" starting in the 1850s. In response, France enacted a trademark law. Brandy companies began registering

TOP SHELF HENNESSY

In addition to VS, VSOP, and XO, Hennessy offers a few noteworthy bottles, not for the faint of heart (or wallet).

🍷 **PRIVATE RESERVE ($150):** In 1873, the Hennessys produced an exceptional cognac for family consumption. The brandy inspired so much enthusiasm in everyone who tasted it, drinkers finally persuaded Gilles Hennessy (the founder's great-great-grandson) to market the stuff. Made of grapes grown in Cognac's most distinguished region—La Grande Champagne—this liquor delivers a floral fragrance and a burst of vanilla, honey, and tobacco flavors.

🍷 **PARADIS EXTRA ($250):** In Cognac, *paradis* refers to the innermost recesses of a brandy cellar, where the finest liquor is stored in great glass jars. Hennessy owns the most famous *paradis* in the world, and it's from here that the firm draws its liquors to blend the Paradis Extra. The mix, which is full-bodied and drenched with flavor, is a marriage of hundreds of different brandies. You can expect plenty of fruit with a touch of pepper on the tongue.

labels and bottling their liquor with their own name on it (as opposed to selling the anonymous casks to importers, who put *their* labels on it).

Today, the choices of cognacs available run the gamut—from the cheap stuff, which is great for mixing (with, say, 7 Up), to $3000 bottles, which literally took a century to create. If you're a guy who could afford a bottle of the latter—a guy like Tupac Shakur, for example—the lesson is clear: drink with pleasure and watch your back. There will always be some thirsty thug lurking in the shadows.

♀ RICHARD HENNESSY ($1500):

The first time I tasted this rare cognac, I turned to the bartender and asked if I could take my pants off. Thank God I wasn't picking up the tab that night (as you can see, this liquor ain't cheap). The blend, a tribute to the firm's founder, has more than one hundred brandies in it, some that have been aging since the early nineteenth century. Every one represents the finest of the brandies distilled during each of the eight generations of the Hennessy family. Complex yet perfectly balanced, Richard Hennessy delivers an explosion of flavors: hazelnut, apricot, a hint of chocolate, etc.

♀ TIMELESS ($3000):

This cognac is so rare, few connoisseurs have ever laid eyes on it. But there are bottles out there. Created in 1999 exclusively for the millennium celebration, the blend marries an exceptional brandy made in each of the decades of the twentieth century. The point: to create a tasty liquor that distills and suspends time. This cognac includes vintages from 1900, 1918, 1929, 1939, 1947, 1953, 1961, 1970, 1983, and 1990. If you ever have the pleasure, consider yourself blessed.

CHAPTER 13

Dom Perignon

EST. BIG SHOTS

"I Am Drinking Stars!"

Champagne is the only wine that leaves a
woman beautiful after drinking it.
—Mademoiselle de Pompadour,
mistress of King Louis XV of France,
mid-eighteenth century

According to one of the greatest myths in the long intoxicating history of booze, champagne was discovered on a fall day some three hundred–plus years ago. In his dank cellar, a blind monk stood tasting a vintage he'd made from grapes picked at different locations around his vineyard in the northern plains of France. Renowned for his eccentric winemaking methods, the blind monk had mixed the different grape bunches like a mad scientist, suffering over the choice of each single ball of fruit. When he scooped some of the potion out of a barrel to inspect it, the wine frothed out of his goblet. He lifted it to his lips and tasted, then cried out to his fellow monks as if he'd just touched the hand of God.

"Come, brothers, hurry!" he shouted. "I am drinking stars!"

The stars, of course, were bubbles of carbon gas in the wine. And the vintner's name was Dom Perignon. Artists have since rendered the winemaker in the typical garb of the Benedictine monk: a long black robe with a large pointed hood, the monk's head tonsured, leaving a halolike ring of hair. He's holding a goblet of glowing golden liquid, which is boiling up out of the cup like a geyser. Perignon's face is clouded by bewilderment, as if he is completely loaded on the stuff.

Of course, you'd have to be loaded yourself to believe this myth is entirely true. Sparkling wine had existed for centuries before Dom Perignon was born. Evidence suggests that the Romans, who first brought viticulture to the Champagne region of France, had experienced the bubbly buzz of sparkling wine. Even the Bible speaks of wine that "moveth."

But Dom Perignon is credited for the discovery to this day, because in the monk's time, a sparkle of carbon gas was considered a fault in a wine. Froth belonged to beer, the drink of the English. Bubbles were considered vulgar, a sign that the grapes used to make the wine weren't quite ripe yet. But by Dom Perignon's death in the year 1715, sparkling wine from his vineyard at the Abbey de Hautvillers was the preferred beverage for the finest tables throughout Europe. By the time Perignon died, according to the diaries of his protégé, Brother Pierre, the French had developed an absolute "mania" for his sparkling wine. "The Reverend Father Perignon achieved the glory of

Dom Perignon discovering champagne. *(Image courtesy of the Mary Evans Picture Library, London)*

giving the wines of Hautvillers the high reputation they enjoy from Pole to Pole," Pierre wrote.

Perignon's eternal fame was secured. He had created a magical wine, rich with effervescent perfection. The wine tasted so good you could sip it right out of a lady's slipper (which, centuries before the shower was invented, must have been quite a feat). Today, the drink is still the toast of dignitaries the world over, from James Bond to Queen Elizabeth. Currently, it's the only wine sold at Hooters restaurants: the "Gourmet Chicken Wing Dinner," twenty wings and a bottle of Dom for $148.88. What an honor.

(Here's another honor worth mentioning, as a short aside: Years ago, on May 30, 1976, this writer got his first drunk on with a bottle of Dom. I was five years old, a few years younger than the vintage itself. It was my parents' tenth wedding anniversary, and they'd cele-brated with a couple ceremonial bottles. The next day, I found a half bottle left in the refrigerator and drank it like it was grape juice, which of course it was. Hours later, my mother was ready to take me to the emergency room. She thought I had a brain tumor, the poor lady. Then she found the empty bottle I'd hidden behind the couch.)

The sparkle in the champagne and the very sweet buzz it gener-ously smears on the soul are just a couple of Dom Perignon's wine-making achievements. In a mouthful, this monk is almost single-handedly responsible for turning wine from the crude drink of the Dark Ages into what we now drink today: a heady fermentation of grapes aged in a labeled bottle, made airtight with a chunk of cork tied on top. Perignon was very likely the greatest winemaker in the history of viti-culture, a history that lasts as long as civilized humankind itself.

Pierre Perignon was born in the parish of Ste. Menehould in the Champagne region of France; he was baptized in the church there on January 5, 1639. It was a quaint, sparsely settled area ninety miles to the west of Paris, speckled with sheep farms and vineyards. When they first brought winemaking to the region, the Romans called the place *campus,* which meant "field," adequately describing the region's flatness. The Gauls later changed the name to Champagne. The soil in the region was rich in chalk and minerals, the remnants of an ancient sea that once covered Europe. By the time Pierre Perignon was born, the land was also rich with the blood of dead Frenchmen. Everyone from Attila the Hun to marauding hooligan Brits had swept through, slaughtering and pillaging with apparent glee. Some say you can still taste the blood salt in the wine grown in Champagne.

Perignon enjoyed a bourgeois upbringing. His father was a judge's clerk who married rich. The boy's future was apparently made. But in the spring of 1657, Perignon swore off his earthly belongings, signed away his inheritance, and entered the monastery of St. Vanne at nearby Verdun.

By any respectable standard, you'd have to be a half-wit to join the order of St. Benedict. Perignon rose at two A.M. The day consisted of nine hours of prayer, seven hours of manual labor, and two hours set aside for reading. He slept in a tiny ten-by-nine-foot room, sans any of the beautiful women who, wine aside, have always been France's greatest export.

The monks had just one indulgence: winemaking. Since the Middle

Ages, they had been the chief viticulturists in Europe. The fermented grape juice was used in ritual ceremony and, more important, was sold for profit. Wine selling was the monks' chief source of income. It paid the bills.

In 1668, at the age of twenty-eight, Perignon was sent to the Abbey of Hautvillers, a few days' journey through the countryside, where he would be *procureur*. In today's terms, *procureur* was CEO, drill sergeant, boss man, and resident ass kicker. He was basically in charge of everything. Some eighty years earlier, Hautvillers had been raided and wrecked in the name of God by Protestants. The Abbey was in shambles. Perignon was put in charge of repairing it to its original grandeur—no easy job, especially for a man not yet thirty years old. With plenty of local laborers and monks under his charge, he had the manpower. He had all the time in the world. He was missing one thing: cash.

Money for Perignon literally grew on trees. Or vines, at least. So in order to make some cash, he set about restoring the Abbey's vineyard first.

Generally speaking, most of the wine produced in Champagne at the time was regarded as swill. Burgundy to the near south produced the good stuff: wines that had a reputation outside the village where they were made. Unlike Burgundy's, Champagne's cooler climate tended to kill off a year's harvest early, so the grapes had to be picked before they were completely ripe. The monks used both red and white grapes—very likely pinot noir, pinot meunier, and chardonnay, the same grapes used in today's champagne. The red ones were picked before the skins could gain a strong pigmentation, so the juice they produced was cloudy and straw-colored. The wine was known as *vin gris* (gray wine). Often it was spiked with brandy to keep it from turning to vinegar before it was drunk.

Perignon's first innovation was to create a winepress that squeezed the juice from the fruit more swiftly. The machine forced the juice from the skins before any of the red pigmentation could seep into it. The result: the first truly white still wine made from red grapes.

In the fields, Perignon urged extreme precision in inspecting and harvesting his grapes. As with most geniuses, he would today be regarded as an incredible tight ass, very likely detested by his field hands. Winemakers at the time planted nearly eight thousand vines to the hectare (2.2 acres). Perignon planted five thousand. Field laborers were hired for the equivalent of a few pennies, a loaf of bread, and three *chopines* of wine (literally, three woman's shoes full) per day. Laborers were forbidden to consume a single grape and were never allowed to eat their bread in the fields, "lest their crumbs get in the wine."

Once, the monk caught a field worker stealing a handful of grape vines. The thief was branded on both arms and sentenced to nine years' hard labor.

Perignon's second brilliant winemaking innovation was to mix grapes from different areas in his vineyard, giving rise to the idea of the cuvée. Blending wines was unheard of at this time. You just took all your grapes and pressed the hell out of them. The idea of the cuvée (literally, a large vat used for fermentation) meant that you could blend your best grapes from different areas to make the finest wine possible—the *cuvée par excellence*, "destined for the tables of the greatest princes in Europe," in the monk's words. Then you could make another grade to sell to locals on the cheap, and then finally a batch of swill with which you could pay your workers. This method allowed the maker to control the quality and consistency of the product, not to mention increase profit. (Today's finer viticulturists do the same. That's one reason why you can buy six different 1999 cabernet sauvignons from Mondavi, with prices ranging from $30 to $125.)

During harvest season in the fall, Perignon had his laborers deliver him samples of grapes in wicker baskets from different areas of his vineyard, which spread out across roughly one hundred acres. The monk set the grapes on the windowsill overnight and tasted them in the morning before he ate breakfast. According to his protégé, Brother Pierre, he would then decide on his blends, "not only according to the flavor of the juice, but also according to what the weather had been like that year—an early or late development, depending on the amount of cold or rain there had been—and according to whether the vines had grown a rich or mediocre foliage."

Gradually, Perignon gained quite a reputation. The more wine from Hautvillers flowed on tables all over France, the more cash began to flow in. Like a sharp entrepreneur, the monk dumped his money back into the vineyard. Slowly, Hautvillers began to take over the countryside. Perignon built a cellar that could accommodate five hundred barrels of aging wine. The stage was set for his ultimate innovation—one that he would stumble onto by mistake.

• • •

According to the legend of Dom Perignon, two traveling monks from Spain en route to Sweden stopped for a respite at Hautvillers one day. Perignon noticed that the Spaniards kept their water in gourds that were stopped by a squishy wooden substance, the likes of which the Frenchman had never seen. The wood was soft, so it could be squeezed and shoved in a small hole, where it would then expand to make the hole airtight. The substance, which the Spaniards called cork, kept their drinking water clean and prevented it from spilling as they were dragged by donkeys for hundreds of miles over bumpy terrain on wooden wheels.

Perignon requested samples of cork from Spain. At this moment, as Richard Fetter points out in his perceptive biography *Dom Perignon: Man and Myth*, the wine export business was born.

Until that time, wine in France was transported in casks. When purchased, it was decanted into fragile bottles and stopped with whittled wood chunks tied down with hemp. Consumers were left with bottles that broke easily and wine that spilled during transportation. Since the bottles weren't airtight, the wine turned to vinegar if it wasn't drunk within a couple weeks.

With corked bottles, wine could be shipped more easily. It could be sent as a finished product throughout Europe and sold to consumers, who wouldn't have to lug around their own bottles. Following Dom Perignon's lead, winemakers all over Europe began bottling their wine, melting wax over their corks to ensure the bottle was genuine, and branding a symbol in the hot wax, the precursor of the wine label. Perignon's symbol was a cross.

There was just one problem. Vintners began to notice that, while their wine aged in bottles, the glass tended to explode. They were bottling the juice before the fermentation process was complete, so the liquid was producing bubbles of carbon gas that, in an airtight bottle as opposed to a wooden cask, had no escape. *Kaboom!* According to records dug up in Hautvillers, 1560 out of 2381 bottles exploded one year in Perignon's cellar. Glass shattered to shards and flakes, and the fruit flies swarmed in. . . . In today's parlance, it would be called a complete fucking mess.

To solve the problem, winemakers began aging their product longer in casks before bottling it. But Perignon, in contrast, took a different route. He began using *verre anglais*—bottles blown from a new, much stronger glass made with technology imported from London. If

"Du Champagne, Avec un Coup de Poing, Monsieur?"

Champagne can be a riddle. Here's a little guide to help you read the label.

GRAND CRU: Champagne made from grapes considered to be of the highest quality (i.e., with a rating of 100 out of 100). Of the nearly three hundred villages in the Champagne region, only seventeen have grand cru ratings. In other words, this is some of the finest wine on the planet.

PREMIER CRU: The next level down from grand cru, this wine is made from grapes grown in villages that have ratings of 90–99. Expect to spend a bundle and to drink a fine bottle.

CUVÉE: The blend. Champagnes today might be a blend of twenty, thirty, even forty different wines.

VINTAGE CHAMPAGNES: A champagne is considered vintage if the head dude at the champagne house feels that the grapes harvested that year are of superior quality. Vintage champagne must be aged at least three years before drinking, though it's often aged much longer.

NONVINTAGE: Three-quarters of the champagne produced is nonvintage. In other words, here's your everyday, deliciously rich sparkling wine. A nonvintage champagne must be aged at least two years prior to drinking.

the wine was bottled at just the right time, the glass was strong enough to prevent explosions during the fermentation process. In order to collect the sediment in the neck, the bottles were aged upside down, stuck neck down in some sand. When one was opened, the carbonic gas would make the cork pop like a musket shot, and the aged wine would then bubble over.

Champagne as we know it was born.

The official year given to the first vintage was 1690, when Dom Perignon was fifty-one years old. Bottles still sometimes exploded, which drove up the price of the ones that didn't. Still, the stuff took off on the burgeoning wine market among customers who could afford it (thus the high-end clientele that champagne has always enjoyed). Within four years, the king of France himself, Louis XIV, had ordered his share of Dom Perignon's wine. A bottle was selling for five times

ROSE: Pink bubbly—great for Valentine's Day and anniversary dinners—has a dash of red wine or red grape skin added into the mix, to darken the color. It's generally full-bodied.

BLANC DE NOIRS: Most champagne is made with pinot noir, pinot meunier, and chardonnay grapes. This slightly pinkish champagne has no chardonnay.

BLANC DE BLANCS: A lighter sparkling wine made exclusively of chardonnay grapes.

BRUT: Dry. A brut wine will have less than 1.5 percent sugar in it.

EXTRA SEC OR EXTRA DRY: Basically the same as brut, though perhaps a tiny bit sweeter.

DEMI-SEC: A sweet champagne, with up to 5 percent sugar.

DOUX: A sweet wine with more than 5 percent sugar. (Doux and demi-sec are considered dessert wines.)

CUVÉE DE PRESTIGE OR CUVÉE SPECIALE: The crème de la crème of champagne brands. Moët & Chandon's Dom Perignon was the first to use this term. Others today include Grand Cuvée from Krug, Belle Epoque from Perrier-Jouët, and Cristal from Louis Roederer.

the price of other regional wines. Champagne was here to stay, and the legend of Dom Perignon was made.

Not long after, the king of France made a law stipulating the exact size and shape of the bottle, which is pretty similar to the Dom Perignon bottle now in stores. It must weigh twenty-five ounces, the king proclaimed. It must contain one Paris pint (1.6 pints), and be tied down with three-threaded string twisted and knotted in the form of a cross over the cork. Voilà! Champagne.

For the rest of his life, the monk worked to perfect the process of making bubbly. According to some accounts, he went blind during these years. (Surely this had nothing to do with all the homemade booze he was drinking.) Nevertheless, his skill in making wine with bubbles increased until the end. It was in essence a guessing game.

"The great art of making champagne consists in seizing the moment when the wine in cask has neither more nor less of the quantity of sugar needed to give an excellent *mousse* [froth] and yet not break the bottles," explained one nineteenth-century wine historian.

By the time Dom Perignon died in 1715, his name was as famous as any in France. He was one of only two monks ever to be buried in the choir of the church at the Abbey de Hautvillers. There his gravestone bears this epitaph:

Here lies
Dom Pierre Perignon
For 47 years
Cellarer of this monastery, who
Having administered the affairs
Of our community
With praiseworthy care,
Full of virtue
Above all in his fatherly love
For the poor
Died
At the age of 77
In 1715
Rest In Peace

So how did the *brand* of Dom Perignon come to be? Not surprisingly, the Dom Perignon you can buy today has nothing to do with the monk, aside from the fact that he is credited with the "discovery" of champagne.

The year was 1932. Alcohol was illegal in the United States when the brand was first launched. In Europe, the wine market was getting spanked, a casualty of the worldwide Great Depression. In order to stimulate sales, the folks at the esteemed champagne house Moët & Chandon decided to produce a cuvée of the finest sparkling wine and name it after the great monk. Three years later, the company sent gift baskets to one hundred fifty of its best clients, mostly English aristocracy, containing two bottles of this rare champagne. The label, almost identical to the one produced today, featured wild grape vines, a big green star, and the name Cuvée Dom Perignon across it in delicate script. The vintage was 1921. If you were to stumble across one of these bottles today, it would be worth hundreds of thousands of dollars.

Word of the fabulous bubbly quickly spread across the Atlantic. With Americans drunk with glee over the repeal of Prohibition, a great demand for the fabled champagne grew in New York City. So in November 1936, Moët & Chandon sent the first shipment of one hundred cases of the 1921 vintage by boat to America. By New Year's Eve of that year, a select few in the New World were getting sloshed on the finest sparkling wine ever produced anywhere in the world.

The vintages of Dom available today are still of extraordinary quality by most experts' opinion. By law, champagne must be from the Champagne region of France and aged at least fifteen months. (Otherwise the drink is just called "sparkling wine".) Unlike in Dom Perignon's day, when the wine's bubbles were a result of the fact that the juice was still fermenting when it was bottled, today's champagne is bottled completely fermented. A dash of sugar is then added to the still wine before corking—touching off a "second fermentation"—to give the stuff its trademark effervescence.

By the way, a bottle of champagne off the shelf contains roughly forty-nine million little bubbles (yes, someone actually took the time to count). And the taste? France exported 262.6 million bottles in 2001, so they must be doing something right. The unique drink has never lost its luster after all these centuries. Spend a sunset with a bottle and a chilled Maine lobster or some delicate oysters with just a drop of lemon or a peanut butter sandwich, if that kind of thing turns you on. Affording a bottle of bubbly is half the pleasure.

PART VI

LAST CALL!

CHAPTER 14

TANQUERAY, CABO WABO, J&B, OLD GRAND-DAD . . .

The Gang's
All Here

🍸 TANQUERAY:

At twenty years old, surely to the chagrin of his parents, one **Charles Tanqueray** abandoned the family practice (he'd come from three generations of clergy in Bedfordshire, England) to start a small gin distillery in the Bloomsbury district of London in 1830. The move paid off. His elixir, an immediate favorite, was eventually given the moniker the "Rolls-Royce of Gin." Thirty-two years later, the Martini was invented, which wasn't exactly bad for sales. One of the gin brand's proudest moments: during U.S. Prohibition, Tanqueray continued legally delivering gin to islands around the mainland in cases designed to float. If they accidentally fell off the boat into the water—*whoops!*—they could easily be "found" by smugglers. Thus Tanqueray enjoyed a healthy presence in speakeasies all over the country. Today, it's the bestselling gin in America.

🥃 OLD GRAND-DAD:

Who the hell's granddad is it anyway? The Old Grand-Dad is **R. B. Hayden**'s granddad. Back in 1840, R. B. Hayden built a state-of-the-art bourbon distillery in Bardstown, Kentucky—the same town where Jim Beam's distillery is located. Hayden's spot was by all means perfect. "The drainage was downhill from the cattle feeding pens and troughs, and so cow manures, both hard and soft, did not get into the mash tub," according to one Hayden relative. Good thing. R. B. named his hooch after his grandfather (thus the "old grand-dad" moniker), who was himself a bit of an icon in the whiskey trade: **Basil Hayden**, one of the forefathers of Kentucky bourbon. Name sounds familiar? Today, Jim Beam is selling a small-batch bourbon under the name Basil Hayden as a tribute to the man. Matter of fact, Beam bought the Old Grand-Dad label as well.

🥃 JAMESON:

This brand of creamy Irish whiskey is the best known in the world, which is bizarre considering the fact that the company didn't start bottling its own branded whiskey until 1968, under the name Jameson Red Seal. Before that time, the whiskey was sold in casks to be bottled and labeled by other companies. First founded by **John Jameson** in Dublin in 1780, Jameson was one of the earliest companies to mass-produce whiskey. Along with his sons, John Jr. and William (thus the JJ&S on the label, for John Jameson and Sons), Jameson was producing whiskey with a 1,508-gallon (read: big) pot still at his premises on Bow Street in Dublin way back in 1810. By 1880, the company was distilling 1.2 million gallons of liquor annually. If you can get your hands on it, try Jameson Gold Special Reserve, a blend of whiskies from eight to twenty years old, some of it aged in American oak bourbon casks and Spanish Oloroso casks.

♆ GORDON'S: This London Dry Gin was one of the

first, founded by **Alexander Gordon** in south London. Gordon was a Scot raised in Glasgow who celebrated his wedding day in 1769 by establishing his liquor biz, Gordon & Company. Tapping an unpolluted water source that he'd found in Clerkenwell, just outside London, Gordon managed great success in a short time. Today, the gin—made from Alexander's exact recipe—is sold in one hundred fifty countries. About a dozen bottles of the stuff are purchased in Great Britain every single minute.

⬜ J&B: The year was 1749. An Italian from Bologna, **Giacomo

Justerini,** fell desperately in love with an opera singer named Margerita Bellino. When Bellino went to London, Justerini followed. The love affair didn't work out. Rather than drinking himself to death, Justerini, whose uncle was a distiller, set up shop as a wine merchant and began buying and blending single-malt whiskies from the north. In 1831, a gentleman named **Alfred Brooks** became a partner in the company. The firm took the name Justerini & Brooks, or J&B (since Justerini didn't sound very British), with headquarters in the prestigious Regents Park section of London. Today, J&B is the fifth best-selling Scotch in the U.S., behind Dewar's, Johnnie Walker Red and Black, and Chivas.

⬜ SAUZA: Second fiddle to Jose Cuervo for two centuries

now, this tasty tequila was first exported by **Don Cenobio Sauza** in 1873. While both families emerged as the front-runners in liquor production in the town of Tequila, Mexico, during the nineteenth century, Cuervo has remained number one—with a single exception: Sauza Hornitos is the bestselling 100 percent blue agave tequila in the world. (*No comprende* 100 percent blue agave? See the sidebar on pages 86–7.)

BALLANTINE: A contemporary of Johnnie Walker, **George Ballantine** opened a shop in Edinburgh in 1827. He sold tea, fish, booze, and women's dirty undergarments. (Just kidding about the undergarments.) At the time, shady liquor dealers were putting all kinds of stuff in the batch so they could increase profits on their dubious whiskies, the same way coke dealers today cut the fine stuff with everything from aspirin to baby powder. Where could a drinker go to get reliable Scotch whiskey in the 1800s? To a reliable shop with a reliable proprietor who happened to be a reliable blender. Like Johnnie Walker, George Ballantine became famous for his delicious blends of single-malt whiskies. His legacy—Ballantine's Finest—can be hard to come by these days, which is a damn shame.

POPOV: There's nothing like a nice warm shot of this juice early in the morning, straight out of the plastic bottle. Go ahead! Grab it and squeeze it like it was a mustard squirter. Fact is, Popov gets this writer's vote for the very worst hooch on the planet—the bottom of the barrel, the Cincinnati Bengals of liquors. As far as the identity of Mr. Popov goes—for surely the liquor is named after somebody— nobody seems to know it. Even a spokesperson at the label's parent company, Diageo, said, "Wow. I have no idea who Popov was." Better off that way.

CHIVAS: Way back in the mid-nineteenth century, **James Chivas** became the owner of a shop in Aberdeen, a busy port town on the east coast of Scotland. With his brother, **John**, he started selling Chivas Brothers' blended whiskies in 1857. Apparently, the brothers were good at blending. Orders started coming in from all over the place, and folks have been drinking Chivas whiskey ever since. For a real treat, try the Rare Old Eighteen Year Old.

CAMPARI: That strange red elixir from Italy, which no one except Euros ever drinks, has sixty ingredients in it. The beverage was invented in 1860 by **Gaspare Campari**, the master bartender at a place called the Bass Bar in Turin. Gaspare's concoction is basically a neutral spirit (alcohol) flavored with all kinds of crazy botanicals. If you're in the mood, the stuff does taste pretty damn good over ice with soda or tonic and a lime. Or try a Negroni: a shot of gin, a shot of Campari, and a shot of sweet vermouth over ice with a lemon twist.

BUSHMILLS: Whether whiskey was in fact invented in Scotland or Ireland, no one is ever likely to know for sure. Whoever tells you they know is lying. That said, both kinds have their distinct flavors and their big names. Bushmills, a distillery in Northern Ireland, owns the oldest license in the United Kingdom (dating back to 1608). Contrary to popular belief in bars across America, the liquor is not named after a man, but a place—a town called Bushmills on the River Bush.

CANADIAN CLUB: No, it's not named after him, but this whiskey's founder, **Hiram Walker**, deserves a paragraph to say the least. Born in Massachusetts in 1816, Walker left the States because of those damn temperance idiots. He opened a distillery in Ontario and, using the profits, later founded his own town, Walkerville. (It's still there, though it's since been incorporated into the town of Windsor.) He established a new distillery in 1884 and called his whiskey Club. In the 1890s, when the U.S. government set up legislation that required liquors to name their provenance right on the label, Walker added the word Canadian to his Club whiskey. When he died in 1899, his obituary in the *Detroit News* waxed thick: "Wherever you ask for American whisky today, in Europe, Asia, or Africa, you are offered not Yankee spirits, but Walker Club."

DON JULIO: Tequila producers always have the coolest names. **Don Julio Gonzalez** opened his distillery in 1942, at the ripe old age of seventeen. He grew up outside the town of Tequila, Mexico, and worked in the industry from childhood on. So it's no surprise that his Don Julio Silver (white tequila that's bottled right out of the still without aging) and Don Julio Anejo (aged in charred casks that give the liquor color and a deeper texture) is tasty stuff. Like all tequila, it can do a tap dance on your vertebrae too. Keep some aspirin by the bed.

RICARD: "It will be called Ricard, the real pastis from Marseille," said twenty-two-year-old **Paul Ricard** upon creating his now famous 90 proof anise-based liquor. (It tastes like licorice juice with an alcoholic snap to it.) In France, Ricard is widely consumed as a before-dinner drink. The ritual: pour a shot in a glass and then add a cup of chilled water and some shaved ice. Voilà. Drink up. How successful has Paul Ricard's pastis become? Paul's son, Patrick Ricard, is now CEO of the parent company Pernod Ricard (the two pastis firms Pernod and Ricard merged in 1975). The company is now the third-largest wine-and-spirit conglomerate in the world, counting among its brands Jameson, The Glenlivet, Wild Turkey, Martell, not to mention Ricard itself.

DEWAR'S: John Dewar started in the booze business working as a cellarman for his uncle, who ran a wine-importing company in Perth, Scotland, in the early part of the nineteenth century. Dewar later founded his own firm in 1846, marketing himself as an expert whiskey blender. By the time he handed over the operation to his sons, **Tommy** and **John**, in the 1880s, the Dewar's name was well-known among drinkers in the Scottish Highlands. Around this time, the Dewar's jug looked much like a life-size sheep's penis, dark brown in color, with the word "Dewar's" tattooed across the base. (Coincidental? Arguably not.) The firm opened an office in London before the end of the century to take on brandy and gin, the fashionable urban drinks at the time. Then it invaded New York, setting up shop on Bleecker Street in 1895. Today, Dewar's is the bestselling Scotch whiskey in the States.

CABO WABO: In comparison to poodle-haired David Lee Roth, former Van Halen front man **Sammy Hagar** is a blithering idiot onstage. No, that's harsh. I take that back. He's not an idiot—he's just blithering. But when it comes to tequila, the guy does know his shit. Hagar teamed up with a small tequila distiller in the Jalisco region of Mexico and launched his brand in 1996. He markets three tequilas: a *blanco* (no aging), a *reposado* (aged up to a year in oak barrels), and an *anejo* (aged up to five years). All of them make the grade. There's a saying, coined by playwright Jean Kerr, that goes like this: "Even though a number of people have tried, no one has ever found a way to drink for a living." It seems as if Hagar's made a damn fine effort proving Kerr wrong. If this book sells a few copies, I'll gladly try to follow in his footsteps, except for the part where I find out that I've been replaced by Gary Cherone from Extreme.

MOUNT GAY: The folks at Mount Gay claim that their distillery is the oldest commercial rum producer in the Caribe, dating back to 1703. That year, a couple British sailors, **William Gay** and

Ensign Abel Gay, purchased an estate in St. Lucy, Barbados. A small pot still was there on the property, already set up to brew molasses into rum. Folks have been guzzling Mount Gay gleefully ever since. A classic summer cocktail: add two parts Mount Gay Refined Eclipse Barbados Rum to one part tonic over crushed ice with a lime. There you have it—paradise.

Acknowledgments

Special thanks go out to a number of liquor historians, whose work I used in addition to various other sources to put together this book: Helen Arthur, Peter C. Newman, Nick Brownlee, Jessica Warner, Hernando Calvo Ospina, Richard L. Fetter, Gilbert Delos, and David Wondrich. Also, I'd like to thank all the liquor companies represented for supplying historical information and images, in particular the folks at Jim Beam, Jose Cuervo, Bacardi, Jack Daniel's, Baileys, Diageo, and Jeffrey Pogash at Schieffelin & Somerset. Thanks also to Lisa Dicker, everyone at the Harvey Klinger agency, and my editor, Ron Martirano. More thanks to K.B., J.K., M.R., and J.M. The final nods go out to Sir Loin, for throwing up on everything *but* my manuscript, and Michelle, for her asparagus risotto and for helping me write this thing.

About the Author

A. J. Baime is currently articles editor for *Playboy* magazine. Previously, he worked for *Boston Magazine* and *Maxim*, where he covered food and beverages, as well as myriad other beats. As a freelancer, Baime has written for *The New York Times Magazine*, *The Village Voice*, *Spin*, *Popular Science*, *Real Simple*, and other periodicals. He has a master's degree in literature from NYU.

DR